D1783169

J. Elihay

English translation: Carol Sutherland, Susan Fogg

Speaking Arabic

A Course in Conversational
Eastern (Palestinian) Arabic

Book 1
Lessons 1-15

Second edition

Minerva Publishing House
2011

Minerva Publishing House

P.O.B 7023 Jerusalem 91070, Israel

www.speaking-arabic.com

Copyright © 2009 by J. Elihay

Reprinted (with corrections) 2011

All rights reserved by the publisher

ISBN 978-965-7397-16-9

Contents

Preface	[1]
Abbreviations and Symbols	[7]
Lesson 1	1
Lesson 2	8
Lesson 3	13
Lesson 4	18
Lesson 5	24
Lesson 6	31
Lesson 7	39
Lesson 8	46
Lesson 9	53
Lesson 10	62
Lesson 11	69
Lesson 12	76
Lesson 13	84
Lesson 14	91
Lesson 15	98
Appendix	106
Key to the Exercises	111
Vocabulary and Rules	125

Preface

This series of books is designed to provide a practical grounding in the colloquial Palestinian dialect of Arabic. The course addresses learners who are not content with a superficial knowledge of the language, but wish to speak fluently and understand what they hear. With this in mind, we have tried to present a broad general survey of the dialect's grammar, sentence structure and word forms, as well as a comprehensive vocabulary. From basic word lists in Book 1 we move on to a more widely ranging vocabulary in Books 2, 3 and 4.

Potential students of Arabic will naturally ask themselves: "Why devote so much time to the colloquial language? And what is it anyway – some kind of slang?" Perhaps they will say to themselves, "I want to learn proper Arabic, not something that's spoken in the street!" This obliges us to describe the special dual nature of the Arabic language.

What is colloquial Arabic?

Colloquial Arabic is the everyday language spoken by all Arabs all the time – in the home, at work, out shopping, etc. It is different from **written** literary Arabic, which is used in books, newspapers and even in family letters, and from the **official** Arabic heard on the radio and TV and in public lectures and speeches. To help clarify this point: When two well-educated people are engaged in everyday conversation – not in front of the microphone or at an official symposium – they will speak colloquial Arabic. On the other hand, a child writing to his or her parents will do so in written / literary (i.e., non-colloquial) Arabic.

The written and colloquial forms of Arabic are two different varieties of the same language. One could almost say that they are two different languages. If you want to talk to Arabs, it's a good idea to learn the spoken – colloquial – form as a separate language with its own individual characteristics. Colloquial Arabic should never be regarded as a "sloppy" or "corrupt" form of the written language that can be improvised at random by leaving off a few word endings. Nonetheless, written and colloquial Arabic do have a great deal in common, including a large shared vocabulary. The degree of kinship becomes clearer the more one learns of both. At first glance, however, it is the differences that are more apparent, and these include:

- Everyday words in the spoken language which don't exist in the written version, and vice versa.
- Words common to both languages, but pronounced differently in each.
- Differences in the conjugation of the verb.
- Differing sentence structures and rules of pronunciation.

Colloquial Arabic is nonetheless influenced by literary Arabic (this will be explained in Book 2), and some people speak a mixture of the two, especially when discussing abstract, technical or official topics, or in television interviews, when they want to adopt a more formal tone and use a higher register of language. This varies from one person to another, and some highly educated people will stick to colloquial speech throughout an interview, or start off with a couple of sentences in the literary language before switching to colloquial.

This is why it is important for you to begin by thoroughly learning colloquial Arabic as it is used in everyday conversation between native speakers. In Books 3 and 4 we shall use recordings from radio and television to help you make the acquaintance of what is known as "educated Arabic," which is a combination of literary and colloquial.

Palestinian Arabic

Throughout the Arab world people speak their local dialects, which vary from country to country. An Egyptian visiting Morocco, for example, will be unable to understand the local people when they speak to one another, though he may be able to identify the odd word here and there.

The colloquial Arabic taught in this book is uniquely Palestinian; however, the Palestinian dialect very closely resembles those of Lebanon and Syria, and it is spoken in Jordan, too, because of the large number of Palestinians who live there. Here and there throughout this course we shall point out similarities between the Palestinian dialect and its near neighbors.

The Palestinian dialect itself is not uniform, and different varieties of it are heard in different parts of the country. People in towns speak differently from those in rural areas; Galileans speak slightly differently from Jerusalemites. In this book we have chosen to teach the **urban dialect**, while indicating the minor differences in usage between the Galilee region (Nazareth, Haifa, etc.) and Jerusalem. Apart from a few words and phrases there is very little dialectal difference between the north and south of the country, and learners will soon grow accustomed to the speech of the area they live in. If you speak the urban dialect taught in this book – with the correct pronunciation, of course – all Arabs will understand you. The individual idiosyncrasies of particular villages or regions (the villages along the Lebanese border, for example, or in the Gaza Strip) can easily be learned through spending time in these areas. The final lesson in the course (Book 4, Lesson 50) is devoted to a study of the differences between Lebanese, Syrian and Palestinian Arabic.

Lesson structure

All the lessons are constructed more or less along the following lines:

1. **Presentation of the main topic** of the lesson (the conjugation of a particular verb, a certain type of sentence structure, etc.) The idea is to help you focus on this specific issue while reading the text.

2. **A vocabulary list** of the new words that appear in the text. These lists will help you with the exercises provided at the end of each lesson.

3. **A conversation** or **story** in Arabic, with a parallel translation into English. This text is designed to provide "real life" examples of the material and vocabulary presented in the lesson, and it is accompanied by **footnotes** containing explanations or related material that will help you remember a particular word or better understand its meaning. If you feel that you are drowning in an excess of new information you can ignore the footnotes if you prefer, especially the first time you go over the material.

4. The text is followed by **explanations** that explore the conclusions to be drawn from it and explain relevant rules by means of examples, summaries, tables, etc.

5. At the end of each lesson there are **exercises** that will enable you to practice the newly-learned material.

   – First exercise: "Translate into English" – this gives you the opportunity to try to understand sentences in Arabic that make use of the words you have learned in that lesson (and in previous ones, too).

   – "Complete the sentence": this exercise, too, requires you to understand sentences in Arabic, and to show that you do so by filling in the missing words.

   – Final exercise: "Translate into Arabic" – translation from English to Arabic, using the new vocabulary and applying the rules you have just learned. This is the most difficult and important of the exercises, as it will help you to make **active** use of what you have learned. Apart from enabling you to **understand** the sentences, the exercises will also teach you to **express yourself** using the Arabic words and expressions you have acquired so far.

Note: This course is designed, first and foremost, to give students a practical knowledge of the rules of the language, to instill instinctive linguistic reactions and to enable learners to construct sentences, move smoothly between tenses and from negative to affirmative, conjugate all verbs competently in every conceivable situation, etc. While learning these skills students will also acquire a basic vocabulary, but – in Book 1 at least – the emphasis is not on learning as many words as possible, as new words can be obtained from the dictionary or by asking a native speaker. Such sources of information, however, will not provide learners with the skills they need to express themselves freely (after all, if you buy a piano you won't be able to play it properly straight away, no matter how many explanations about notes and rhythm you may hear. Long hours of practicing scales are required before the theory "comes out through the fingers").

How to use this course

First of all – please note that one of our lessons is not the equivalent of an hour's study in the classroom. Rather, it is a study unit that can be spread out over a longer period of time (two or three days or more).

We recommend the following method of study, which can be adapted to suit everyone as long as you stick to a number of basic principles:

a) Read the beginning of the lesson so you can see what's on the agenda and what new things you're about to discover. You can skip the **Vocabulary** list and go straight to the **Conversation.** Go back and look at the vocabulary whenever you are doubtful about the meaning of a word or want to check its plural form.

b) Read the text silently to yourself while listening to the recording. At this stage you should try only to understand what you are hearing (you can glance at the English translation). After you've listened to the text – or to part of it, if it's divided into a number of sections – do the same thing over again, but this time repeat each sentence **out loud,** trying to imitate the readers' pronunciation and intonation. You can repeat a sentence several times, beating out the rhythm of the stressed syllables on the table.

c) Go over the **Explanations** that follow the text. Read **out loud** the examples they contain, especially the sentences that appear **inside the boxes**, as these summarize the rules you have just learned.

d) Go back to the text, read the **English** silently to yourself and try to translate it back into Arabic – i.e., try to reconstruct the Arabic text without looking at the left-hand column. This will show you all the things you didn't notice on first reading. You can do this while listening to the recording, with your finger on the *pause* button: after you say a sentence, release the button and the reader will tell you what you should have said.

If you've got the sentence right you'll feel validated and encouraged. And if you've made a mistake, you'll hear it corrected at once and realize what you've forgotten or what you didn't understand on the previous reading.

e) At this point you're ready to do the exercises. This doesn't mean that you have to do them all at once without taking a short break (or even a long one....) As we've already said, you can spend two or three days on a single lesson. On the second day it's a good idea to review the text and the explanations so as to refresh your memory before you start on the exercises.

Remember: It's better to learn in short, frequent bursts than spend a long time on a single lesson. In other words, it's better to devote **15 minutes a day** (or, better still, twice a day) to the course rather than two consecutive hours once a week. Success lies in the number of "doses" of the course you take – a daily dose is best!

A little more advice

There's no need to toil over each lesson until you're familiar with every single word and detail. It's better to **move on** to the next lesson and discover new things. You can always go back and re-read anything you've learned and partially forgotten. In any case, doing the exercises, which contain words not just from the current lesson but from earlier ones, too, will mean you have to look back at earlier material or use the index at the back of the book.

Don't worry too much about "rules" and theory. There's no need to learn rules and explanations off by heart. Repeating a sentence like *"When a word that ends in a consonant precedes a word that begins with two consonants, a helping vowel is inserted before the second word,"* won't help you much when you want to speak! The explanations are provided to satisfy your curiosity and so that you'll understand 1) what's happening and 2) when it happens, and why.

The dry theoretical formulation of each rule is followed by a number of examples that illustrate how it operates. If you **repeat these examples out loud**, you will most likely manage to internalize the rule. If you can't take it all in at once, don't worry: every lesson, apart from providing new material, **goes back over rules from previous lessons**, and illustrates their use once again in new sentences. This means that material not absorbed in one lesson will sink in with time, thanks to constant repetition.

The correct pronunciation

As this is a spoken language, proper pronunciation of the words and sentences is crucial. The accent in which a particular language is spoken is like the color of a person's hair or eyes – in other words, it's part of the "personality" of the language. Sloppy pronunciation is like ignoring what is special about a person. And there's another reason why you should make the effort: incorrect pronunciation of Arabic can sometimes cause serious misunderstandings. So do your very best to pronounce the language correctly.

Don't say: "It's impossible, I'll never manage it." An accent isn't something you can get right first time. It's something you'll acquire only after prolonged effort. You will find yourself suddenly able to produce some of the sounds after hearing them in a fresh context (in a new phrase, for example) or when pronounced clearly by a specific speaker; others will require daily practice to accustom the throat or the tongue to the production of new sounds, just as unpracticed fingers require training on the strings of a guitar. All this takes time **and prolonged effort.**

Recordings

Each book is accompanied by a recording of the text of the conversations, together with examples from the explanations and comments, where necessary. The readers are native speakers of Arabic from Galilee and the Jerusalem area – men, women and children.

Although the recordings do not contain everything printed in the book, **all the conversations** are there, together with **examples** from the explanations that precede and follow them. All examples that figure in the recordings are marked in the margin with the sign ■.

Structure of the recorded lessons: musical excerpt on the Arab flute (n**ā**y)

♫♪	three notes	**the name** (and beginning) **of the lesson**
♫	two notes	**conversation**
♪	one note	**explanations**

Abbreviations and symbols

active part.	active participle: *doing / having done*
adj	adjective
adv	adverb
attached pron	attached pronoun: -ni, -ak, -na, -kom…
coll	collective noun
construct	the construct state
cp	comparative adjective, adjective (e.g., bigger). When such an adjective is placed before the noun it denotes the superlative (biggest).
f or fem	feminine.
f sing	feminine singular
f pl	feminine plural
G	Galilee
in s.a.	in some areas
intrans	intransitive
J	Jerusalem
lit	literally
m or masc	masculine
m pl	masculine plural
m sing	masculine singular
m/f	masculine / feminine
n	noun
passive part.	passive participle: *written, done*, etc.
pl	plural
prep	preposition
pron	pronoun
subj	subjunctive, i.e., the present-future tense without b-.
trans	transitive
‿	links two words, to indicate that they have to be pronounced together; in this respect they may be viewed as a single unit: w**ɑ**rɑ‿l-w**a**lad is pronounced as w**ɑ**-rɑl-w**a**-lad (*behind the boy*); š**u**ft‿^{e}kt**ī**r = š**u**f-tek-t**ī**r (*I've seen a lot*) '**i**nte‿kb**ī**r = '**i**n-tek-b**ī**r (*you* ^{m} *are big / old*)
+	with the addition of (the word or suffix following this sign).

± plus-or-minus, i.e., with-or-without (the word that follows). That is to say, the word that follows this symbol may be added or left out without any change of meaning – both versions are acceptable.

= is equal to ...

≠ different from

→ becomes ... / changes into ... / the result of this combination is... e.g., wαrα + -ha → wαrā-ha.

/ precedes an alternative form

// The word preceding this symbol is used in Galilee, the word following it is used in Jerusalem: ’issa // halqēt (*now*) = ’issa in Galilee, halqēt in Jerusalem.

[ ] Square brackets are used for a variety of purposes:

a) After a noun in Arabic the plural form of the same noun is given in square brackets. As the plural forms vary greatly, the singular and plural forms for each noun should be learned together, e.g., madrase [madāres] (*school*); bēt [byūt] (*house*).

b) The 3rd person masculine singular subj.form of the verb is given in square brackets, immediately after the corresponding form in the past tense, e.g., šāf [išūf] *to see* Literally *he saw [that he may see].*

c) Within the English translation of an Arabic text, square brackets enclose one or several words in English which are not represented in the Arabic, but which are necessary to complete the text in English, e.g., muš‿^{e}mnīḥ = *[That's] not good!*

< > These symbols enclose the literal English translation of an Arabic sentence when the corresponding idiomatic English expression contains words different from those used in Arabic. The reader should not be disconcerted by the rather odd forms of English sometimes used in these literal translations: they are intended to imitate the structure and content of the Arabic sentence as closely as possible, in order to help the reader understand every word in it. See examples p.19.

- The hyphen is used to distinguish between the various sections of the Arabic words, e.g., katab-ha (*he wrote it*), so that the reader can understand their construction (in this case, verb + attached pronoun) and pronounce them properly: darasha might be misread as *da-ra-sha* with the English *sh* sound, whereas daras-ha makes things clearer.

#		This sign is reminiscent of the sharp sign in musical notation. Just as the sharp sign in music indicates a rise in pitch, so, in this course, this sign indicates a rise in the style of the conversation, i.e., a higher register of speech. It is used to indicate educated speech, speech above the level of everyday conversation, and words borrowed from literary Arabic.

The alphabet - the consonants

This section can be read as a preliminary to study, in order to obtain an overall picture of the sounds and how they should be pronounced. It is also intended for later reference, as required.

The Arabic alphabetical order is (from left to right)

ء	ا	ب	ت	ث	ج	ح	خ	د	ذ	ر	ز	س	ش
’	_	b	t	ṯ	j	ḥ	ђ	d	ḏ	r	z	s	š

ص	ض	ط	ظ	ع	غ	ف	ق	ك	ل	م	ن	ه	و	ي
ṣ	ḍ	ṭ	ẓ	c	ġ	f	q	k	l	m	n	h	w	y

In this pronunciation guide the letters are arranged in the order of the letters of the English alphabet, so as to make them easy to look up. Note, however, one exception: the ^{c}, which has no English equivalent, appears here as the first letter of the alphabet.

c	A guttural sound produced from the very bottom of the throat, e.g., **ma**^{c}i (*with me*), **ka**^{c}ke (*cake*). Goats say **mā**^{c}.

’	The glottal stop (known in Arabic as “hamza”). This is the sound made by a speaker of English just before beginning to say a word that begins with a vowel: it is the little explosion of air that precedes the pronunciation of words like *enough, altogether, onward,* or *I owe you* (’ay ’ow yu). In certain dialects of English this sound can occur in the middle of a word, as in the Cockney or Glasgow pronunciation of *bottle.* In Arabic the glottal stop can appear anywhere in the word – at the beginning, in the middle or at the end – and it is always clearly heard, e.g., bt**i**s’al = bt**i**s-’al (*you ask*); min **’ē**š (*from what?*), jar**ī**’ = ja-r**ī**-’e (*courageous*); never bti -sal or mi-naish or jari.

a See **Vowels** below.

b As in English, e.g., **bāb** (*door*)

d As in English, e.g., **dāyman** (*always*).

d̲ The English voiced *th*, as in *they, wither.* This sound is rarely heard in urban speech, where it is usually replaced by a -d or a -z.
hād̲a (rural), hāda (urban) = *this* (*one*).
d̲aki (rural), zaki (urban) = *clever; intelligent.*

ḍ An emphatic *d* sound, pronounced with the tip of the tongue pressed against the upper teeth and the back of the tongue touching the palate, e.g., ḍɑllēt (*I stayed*).

e See **Vowels** below

f As in English, e.g., fūt! (*come in!*)

ġ To the English ear this sounds rather like a uvular Parisian *r*, or the sound produced when starting to gargle, e.g., ġāli (*dear, expensive*).

h As in English. In Arabic, however, a *h* sound can occur in final position, e.g., bišbah (*he is similar*), in which a *h* sound can clearly be heard at the end of the word

h The same as *h* above, but practically silent. Used only at the end of a word: tarakūh (*they left him*).

ḥ A strongly emphatic *h* produced by expelling the air through a narrowed throat, e.g., maḥall (*place, room*). Reminiscent of the sound of a dog panting.

ḫ The *ch* sound of the Scots word *loch,* the Welsh *bach* or the German *Nacht.* e.g., ḫalla (*he left; he let*).

i See **Vowels** below.

j In urban speech this is pronounced like the *zh* of *Zhivago,* the French *j* of *joli, Jacques,* and the sound in the middle of the word *pleasure.* In rural speech it is the same as the English *j* of *jump, jolly,* e.g., jāb il-jarīde (*he brought the newspaper*).

k As in English, e.g., kamān

l This is the "clear" English *l* of words like *lean, light* and of French words like *ville.* Occasionally the -l- may be emphatic, as in the word 'ɑllɑ̄h (*Allah*). This emphatic l is pronounced like the "dark" English l of words like *fall, milk.*

m As in English

n As in English, e.g., 'insān (*man, human being*).

o See **Vowels** below.

p As this consonant does not exist in Arabic, most foreign loan-words are pronounced with a *b* instead of a *p*: **blastik** (*plastic*). Occasionally, however, the original *p* is heard, e.g., jipp (*jeep*).

q In urban speech (e.g., in Jerusalem, Haifa, etc.), this letter is pronounced like consonantal ', i.e., as a glottal stop or catch that clearly divides one syllable from the next: bαqαr (*cattle*) is pronounced bα'αr; il-qalb (*the heart*) is pronounced il-'alb; maqlūb (*upside down*) is pronounced ma'-lūb. The Druze say q̈ as in literary Arabic, while the Bedouin say g (bαgαr; il-galb). These variations are worth remembering, as an understanding of them will help you interpret the different types of speech you may encounter. Students themselves should, however, stick to the urban pronunciation.
Note: Since q is pronounced like ', when you hear the sounds 'ar, 'im, remember that when you consult a dictionary you may have to look under both 'ar and qar, 'im and qim in order to find the right word.

q̈ Certain words borrowed from literary Arabic are pronounced with a q̈ even by urban speakers, e.g., musīq̈α (*music*), mαq̈ᾱle (*[newspaper] article*), etc. The q̈ is produced by making a *k* sound as far back in the throat as possible. Like the emphatics, the q̈ affects the surrounding vowels, making them "dark". See below, under ṣ.

r A rolled *r*, as in Scots *burn*, Italian *Roma*

s As in English *simple, master, less.*

ṣ An emphatic *s* sound, pronounced with the tip of the tongue behind the lower teeth and the middle of the tongue touching the palate. When pronouncing this and the other emphatics, the tongue is kept low and spread out so that it feels "thick" and fills the mouth. Emphatic consonants affect the quality of the surrounding vowels, pushing them further back in the mouth and making them "dark" (i.e., α rather than a - see below, in Vowels). This works in reverse, too: if you can manage to pronounce a back α rather than a front a after your emphatics, they will sound much more convincing, even when you don't get the consonants themselves quite right.

š English *sh*, as in *sherry, sham*

t As in English.

ṯ The English unvoiced *th,* as in *thing, thought.* This sound is rarely heard in urban speech, and is used only in words borrowed from literary Arabic, e.g., ṯaq̈ᾱfe (*education, culture*), ṯiq̈α (*trust, faith*).

ṭ An emphatic *t* sound, pronounced with the tip of the tongue pressed against the upper teeth and the back of the tongue touching the palate.

u See **Vowels** below.

w As in English.

y As in English. Note that when -y follows a vowel, the two sounds are pronounced separately, i.e., -ay rhymes with *my*, not with *bay*.

z As in English.

ẓ An emphatic z sound, pronounced with the tip of the tongue behind the lower teeth and the back of the tongue touching the palate, e.g., ẓ**ɑ̄**beṭ (*officer*).

The vowels

In order to indicate the numerous and varied vowels of spoken Arabic, we have adopted the following method of transcription:

a A "front" *a* resembling the Lancashire pronunciation of the word *cat,* the French *papa,* and the German *satt,* e.g., j**a**mal (*camel*), k**a**tab (*he wrote*).
Bold **a** is the same sound stressed, and **ā** is the same but longer.

ɑ A "back" a - the *ah* sound of the English *car* or the French *âne,* but short, e.g., ṭ**ɑ**lɑb (*he requested*), m**ɑ**rɑḍ (*illness*). This is the "dark" *a* often heard before or after an emphatic consonant or an r (see above, under ṣ). **ɑ̄** is the same, but longer.

e A short *eh* sound, as in the English *egg, send, led,* e.g., w**ā**led (*father, parent*), ḫ**ā**tem (*ring*).

ᵉ Same as the above, or even shorter. This vowel is not part of the word as such, but is popped in between two consonants to make pronunciation easier. It can never be stressed.
Examples: '**i**bᵉn (*son*), btik**ᵉ**tbu (*you write*).

ē A very long *eh* sound, somewhere between the English *met* and *meet*.
It resembles a long French *é* or the German *Mehl, Seele,* e.g., w**ē**nak (*where are you?*), sant**ē**n (*two years*).

i A short *i* sound, as in English *bit, miss,* e.g., b**i**nt (*daughter; girl*), '**i**smak (*your name*).

ī A long *ee* sound, as in English *meet, feet,* e.g., mud**ī**r (*manager*), Sal**ī**m (a first name).

o A short vowel somewhere between the *oh* of *from* and the *oo* of *hook,* like the French *bientôt,* or the German *Stroh,* e.g., ḥ**o**bb (*love*) is pronounced as something between ḥobb and ḥoobb; in banāt-kom (*your daughters*), -kom is a sound between *intercom* and *-koom*.

o   A short *oh* sound. This vowel functions like ᵉ above, e.g., ḍuhᵒr (*noon*), šuġᵒl-na (*our work*), btumᵒrqu / btumrᵒqu (*you pass by*).

ō   The same sound as 'o' above, but longer. The Arabic word lōn (*color*) sounds like the French *cône, faune,* or the German *Lohn.*

u   A short oo as in the English word *roof*, e.g., muftāḥ (*key*).

ū   A longer oo as in *lose, loot* or the exclamation *coo!* For example, fūt! (*come in!*).

Stress

The stressed vowel is indicated by a **bold** character, e.g., ma**d**rase (*school*), ma**ḥ**allo (*his place*). You must bear in mind that a stressed syllable is not necessarily a long syllable. **za**lame (*human being / person*) is composed of three short syllables, the first of which is stressed.

Long vowels are indicated by a line over the top of the vowel, e.g., bāb (*door*), kamān (*also*), wēn (*where*).

Getting vowel length and stress right is very important, as both contribute greatly to the rhythm of the sentence, and help ensure that you will be understood.

id-dars[1] il-'awwal

1

The First Lesson <the lesson the first>

Let's begin by getting to know a few words, then we'll dive straight into a simple conversation. After you've read it we can summarize what you've learned from it.

Vocabulary

mīn	who?	šū, šu	what?
wēn	where?	hōn	here
bint	daughter, girl	bēt	house
'ana	I	miš, muš	not, [is] not
'ā / 'aywa	yes	la'	no
na^{c}am	yes	ḥilu	beautiful
hal-	this, these; that, those (used before both m and f nouns)		
hāda	this/that^{m}	kbīr	big
hāy / hādi	this/that^{f}	sāken	lives / living^{m} (in a place)
'inte ('inta^{J})	you$^{m\ sing}$	sākne	lives / living^{f} (in a place)
'inti	you$^{f\ sing}$	kamān	also, too, as well; else
il- / l-	the	mudīr	manager, boss
u- / w-	and	fi	in, inside; at
ya / yā	oh…! hey…! used before the name or title of the person you're talking to, as in *Oh George, could you tell me…*)		

Conversation

– mīn hāda?	– Who [is] that^{m}?
– hāda Jōrj, il-mudīr.	– That [is] George, the manager.
– u-mīn hāy?	– And who's that^{f} [with him]?
– hāy Maryam binto.	– That's Maryam, his daughter.
– hāy bint il-mudīr? – 'ā.	– That's the manager's daughter? – Yes.
– šū hāda? – hāda bēt.	– What's that? – That's a house.
– bēt mīn?	– Whose house <house [of] who>?

---

1. Why not il-dars? You'll find out why in Lesson 2.

– bēt Jōrj, bēt il-mudīr.	–[It's] George the manager's house <[the] house-of George, the house-of the manager>
– mīn sāken fi hal-bēt	– Who lives in that house?
– Jōrj sāken hōn fi bēto.	– George lives there <here> in his house.
– mīn kamān sāken fi bēto?	– Who else <who also> lives in his house?
– Maryam kamān sākne hōn.	– Maryam lives there <here> too.

The next day George is standing alone in front of his house:

– ya Jōrj, Maryam fi bētak?	– Hello, George <oh George>, is Maryam at home <Maryam in your house>?
– la', Maryam 'issa[2] / halqēt muš hōn.	– No, Maryam's not here at the moment <Maryam now not here>.
– hal-bēt‿^{e}kbīr[3]!	– It's a big house <this house big>.
– 'ā, ^{e}kbīr u-ḥilu.	– Yes, big and very nice <beautiful>.
– ya Jōrj, hāda bētak?	– George, [is] that your house?
– na^{c}am hāda bēti.	– Yes, that's my house.
– bētak ḥilu w-^{e}kbīr kamān.	– It's a nice house, and big, too <your house is beautiful and big too>
hāda bēt‿^{e}jdīd?	Is it a new house <this is a new house>?

---

2. In Galilee the word 'issa is used for *now*, while in Jerusalem people say halqēt. In Lesson 6 we'll learn a word that's used all over the country.

3. il-bēt + kbīr = il-bēt‿^{e}kbīr. A helping vowel is added here between the final -t of the word bēt and the -kb at the beginning of the word kbīr. When exactly does this happen? We'll find out in the next lesson.

– ’**a**ywa, u-**i**nte, w**ē**n b**ē**tak? – Yes. And where do **you** live? <and you, where’s your house>

– ’**a**na? b**ē**ti fi ḥ**ē**fa. – Me <I>? My home’s in Haifa.

– ’**i**nta[J] s**ā**ken fi ḥ**ē**fa? – Do you live <you live> in Haifa?

– ’**a**ywa, ’**a**na s**ā**ken fi ḥ**ē**fa. – Yes, I live in Haifa.

– ḥ**ē**fa mad**ī**ne kb**ī**re u-ḥ**i**lwe kam**ā**n. – Haifa’s a big town, and it’s beautiful, too <and beautiful too>.

– ṭɑyyeb, bik**a**ffi. – OK <good>, that’s enough.

Explanations

1. The verb *to be*

Let’s start with some good news: you don’t have to learn the **present tense** of the verb *to be* in Arabic, because it doesn’t exist (though it does exist in the past and future tenses). Instead of saying, as you would in English, *That’s good*, *I’m here*, *What’s that*? or *You’re tired*, in Arabic you just say *That good*, *I here*, *What that?* and *You tired.* If you take another look at the conversation above you’ll see that the sentence ḥēfa madīne kbīre <Haifa town big> translates into English as *Haifa’s a big town.*

2. The indefinite article

There is no indefinite article in Arabic:

bēt = *house / a house* bēt‿ekbīr = *a big house*

3. Masculine and feminine

In Arabic, objects, as well as people, can be either masculine or feminine. Nouns ending in -e (madīne) are feminine, and both the adjective and some verbal forms change to agree with a feminine noun by adding -e:

kbīr + -e = kbīre[f] *(big)*

ḥilu +-e = ḥilwe[f] *(beautiful, nice)*

sāken + -e = sākne[f] *(live, living)*. Note that the -e between the -k and the -n drops when the feminine ending is added. We’ll explain later why this happens.

Note: There is no need for you to memorize explanations like the one above, as they are provided merely to satisfy your curiosity. With practice you will find that all the grammatical peculiarities described above become second nature.

4. The adjective

In Arabic the adjective is placed **after** the noun:

b**ē**t‿ejd**ī**d	*a new house*
mad**ī**ne kb**ī**re	*a big town*

5. The personal pronouns

Note that the second person (*you*) has both a masculine and a feminine form:

I	**'a**na
you [m sing]	**'i**nte, or **'i**nta [J]
you [f sing]	**'i**nti
he	h**u**wwe, h**ū**
she	h**i**yye, h**ī**

6. The attached pronouns

If you look at the conversation again, you'll see that the word *my* is expressed in Arabic by adding -i to the end of a word: b**ē**ti means *my house. Your, his* and *her* are expressed in the same way. Note that *your* has two forms, one for addressing a male, the other for addressing a female. The following are the appropriate suffixes:

my [m / f]	-i
your [m sing]	-ak
your [f sing]	-ek
his	-o
her	-ha

7. Negation

The word la' means *no* (J**ō**rj s**ā**ken h**ō**n? – **la**'!).

The word muš / miš means *not*.

Do you live here?	– **'i**nte s**ā**ken h**ō**n?
No, I don't (= do **not**) *live here.*	– **la**', **'a**na muš s**ā**ken h**ō**n.
Is the manager's house beautiful?	– b**ē**t il-mud**ī**r **ḥ**ilu?
No, the manager's house isn't (= is **not**) *beautiful.*	– **la**', b**ē**t il-mud**ī**r miš **ḥ**ilu.

Note: Because Arabic has no present tense of the verb *to be*, muš / miš often translates into English as *am not, isn't* or *aren't.* It can also mean *don't* or *doesn't.*

Note: Although **la'** can nearly always be translated as *no* and muš / miš as *not*, there are a few exceptions to this, e.g.,

'**a**na **la**'! = *I'm not* < I no >!

The basic rule is that muš / miš is used to negate a noun (*not a child*), an adjective (*not nice*), an adverb (*not quickly*) or a pronoun (*not you*), while **la'** usually stands alone or, as in the example above, with just one other word.

8. Possessives

English expresses the possessive by using the word *of* or by adding the suffixes *'s* or *s' (the house of the prince / the prince's house*; *the princes' house*). Arabic has no special words or suffixes to express possession: it simply puts the noun denoting the thing possessed immediately in front of the noun denoting the possessor:

b**ē**t J**ō**rj	*George's house*
b**ē**t il-mud**ī**r	*the manager's house* <[the] house [of] the manager>

Note that when the definite article is used in this possessive construction it appears **only before the second of the two nouns**.

9. Questions

English often reverses the order of words or adds the word *do / does* to turn a statement into a question:

That's (that is) your house → Is that your house?

Colloquial Arabic doesn't do this. It relies on the intonation of the voice to indicate whether a sentence is a statement or a question:

h**ā**da b**ē**ti	*That's* <that> *my house.*
h**ā**da b**ē**tak?	*Is that your house* <that [is] your house>?
'**a**na s**ā**ken fi ḥ**ē**fa	*I live in Haifa.*
'**i**nte s**ā**ken fi ḥ**ē**fa?	*Do you live in Haifa?*

10. Pronunciation

As we said in the Preface, it is very important to try to pronounce Arabic properly from the outset. In this lesson, you should pay special attention to the following points:

A long vowel is indicated by a line over the top of the vowel:

s**ā**ken is pronounced **sā**-ken and not s**a**-ken.

Be sure to distinguish between a and α

■ 'ᾱ ≠ 'aywa – ṭαyyeb ≠ sāken (see page [12])

Take care to ensure that doubled consonants really do sound double: in the word 'issa the -s is doubled, i.e., longer and louder. Listen to the recording to hear exactly how it should sound. Practice by pronouncing English combinations such as *Miss Soames, got time, bed down.*

Now would be a good time to reread the lesson or listen to the recording, before you move on to the exercises

Exercises

A. Translate into English:

1. hāda bēt‿ejdīd u-hāda kamān bēt‿ejdīd.
2. mīn sāken fi bētak?
3. 'inte kamān sāken hōn?
4. hāda muš‿ekbīr.
5. mīn kamān sāken hōn?

B. Complete the sentences:

(Replace the English words with the appropriate expression in Arabic):

6. 'inte sāken fi ḥēfa? 'ana (too) sāken fi ḥēfa.
7. Jōrj fi bētak? – (No), Jōrj (isn't) fi bēti.
8. hāda (is new)? – (No), hāda muš (new).
9. binto (lives) fi bēt‿ejdīd, u-bintak (also) sākne (in a new house).

C. Translate into Arabic:

10. I live at the manager's house.
11. You[f sing] don't live here.
12. The house isn't nice.
13. Who's that[f sing]?
14. Isn't that your[m sing] daughter <this not your daughter>?
15. No, that's not my daughter.
16. Maryam, where's your daughter?
17. The boss isn't at your[m sing] house.
18. This is a beautiful town.
19. His daughter isn't beautiful.
20. That's not new!

To make sure you've got everything right, look up the **Key to the Exercises** on page 111.

Don't be content with just writing out the exercises! Read your translations out loud – after you've corrected them, of course!

id-dars it-tāni

2

The Second Lesson <the lesson the second>

In this lesson we shall extend the use of the suffixes -i, -ak, -ek, -o and -ha, which we studied in the first lesson. These suffixes can be added to prepositions (*with, at the home of*, etc.); they can also be attached to the word **wēn** (*where*): **wēnak** means *Where [are] you*?

Vocabulary[1]

kīf	how?	bass	only; but
ᶜind / ᶜand	at, by (as in *how's by you?*); at the home of		
ᶜindi	I have, I've got; at my house, at home		
ᶜindak	you^m have, you've got; at your house, at home		
fīʰ	there is, there are		
ma fī-š	there isn't, there aren't	walad	boy, child
mā fīʰ / fišš	there isn't, there aren't	yaᶜni	that's to say
kull	every, each; all	šuġel // šuġol[2]	work, job
ḥāl	situation, state	mαbsūṭ^m	pleased, feeling well
mαẓbūṭ^m	right, true	jᾱr	neighbor
'iši	thing, something	mαṣᾱri	money

Conversation

– ṣαbᾱḥ il-ḫēr, ya Jōrj.	– Good morning, <morning of goodness>, George!
– ṣαbᾱḥ in-nūr, ya Fahīm.	– Good morning, <morning of light>, Fahim!
– kīf ḥālak?	– How are you <how [is] you situation>?
– 'αllα isallmak[3]	– Fine, thank you < God save you>.
kīf 'inte?	How are you <how you>?
– mαbsūṭ, il-ḥamdi-lla[4]	– Fine <feeling well> thank you <praise to God>.
– u-kīf šuġlak?	– And how's work <your work>?

---

1. Not all new words used in the **Conversation** appear in this list, as their meaning will be clear from the translation provided on the opposite side of the page.
2. See pp. [10] and [11] for the proper pronunciation of the letters ġ and š.
3. This will be explained later. To a woman one says **'αllα isallmek.** Note the difference in pronunciation between **α**-α and **a**-a.
4. This is a contraction of the literary Arabic expression **il-ḥamdu lillāh** <praise to God>.

– yaᶜni[5]… il-yōm iš-šuġᵒl hēk.	– So-so… These days work's… like that <today work's… thus>.
fīʰ šuġᵒl yaᶜni[6],	I mean, I've got work <it means there is work>
bass ma fišš maṣāri.	but I haven't got any money < but there's no money>.
– maẓbūṭ, hēk id-dinya‿l-yōm.	– That's right, that's the way things are these days < thus [is] the world today>.
– u-kīf ᶜindak?	– And how are things with you <how at you>?
–'ana? ᶜindi šuġᵒl u-šuġl‿ᵉmnīḥ.	– Me? I've got a job, and a good job [too].
– ᶜindak bēt kamān u-kull 'iši, hāda mnīḥ. u-kīf jārak 'abu Yūsef?	– You've got a house, too, and everything. That's good. And how's your neighbor, Abu Yusef?
– jāri? hū kamān ᶜindo šuġᵒl u-maṣāri.	– My neighbor? He's got <he too there is at him> work - and money, too.
– bass 'ana ma ᶜindī-š u-ᶜindi ulād - walad u-bint (binᵉt)[7].	– But **I** haven't! And I've got children - a boy and a girl.
– wēn il-binᵉt?	– Where's the girl?
– binti? hiyye fi‿l-bēt halqēt.	– My daughter? She's at home now.
– u-wēn il-walad?	– And where's the boy?
– il-walad kamān fi‿l-bēt.	– The boy's at home <in the house>, too.

Explanations

Let's classify the new things we've discovered in this chapter:

1. The definite article il- and its various forms

We'll start by following the adventures of the word il-, which means *the*.

1. The i- drops whenever il- follows a word ending in a vowel:
   il-bēt → fi‿l-bēt / fi-l-bēt (*in the house; at home*)
   il-yōm → huwwe fi ḥēfa‿l-yōm (*He's in Haifa today*).

---

5. yaᶜni generally means *that's to say…, [I] mean…,* but here it's used to mean *so-so* or *[it] could be better.*

6. That's right, the syllable yaᶜ is unstressed here. Just accept this as a fact for the present (it has to do with the overall intonation of the sentence). You will come across other similar cases which will be explained at the end of this book.

7. Why have we sometimes written bint and sometimes binᵉt, sometimes šuġl and at other times šuġᵒl? You'll find the explanation in the next lesson.

2. In this lesson we've seen that il- can change in other ways, too:

il- + **nūr** = in-**nūr**

il- + **d**inya = id-**d**inya

(like **id-dars** in the title of each lesson in this book)

il- + **š**u**ġ**ol = iš-**š**u**ġ**ol

Conclusion: the -l of il- sometimes turns into the letter that follows it. However, this doesn't always happen:

– It occurs only before the letters d, ḍ, d̲; t, ṭ, t̲ ; n; s, ṣ, z, ẓ, š; r.

These are called the "sun letters" because *sun* – **š**ams – is one of the words before which il- changes its form.

Note: Some people change the form of il- before the letter j-, too, so you will hear both il-j**ɑ̄**r and ij-j**ɑ̄**r.

How can you remember which letters make il- change its form? There's no need to memorize the list above.[8] It's enough to know that the phenomenon exists and to read all the lessons out loud. As you come across more and more examples you will find that, with the help of a few exercises, you start to make the necessary changes automatically.

The definite article in English and in Arabic: Arabic sometimes uses the definite article where English doesn't. When we make a generalization in English, such as *children go to school*, we don't put the definite article *the* before either noun. In Arabic, however, we have to say *the children go to the school* even when we're speaking generally, with no specific children in mind.

---

8. For anyone who does want to try to memorize the list: as a rule, the consonants that cause il- to change are *dentals*, which are pronounced with the tip of the tongue touching the top teeth (d,t,n), sibilants (s,z,š) and the letter r.

2. Helping vowels

Let's go back to another peculiarity of colloquial Arabic which we encountered in the first lesson: il-bēt-ᵉkbīr / il-bēt‿ᵉkbīr

When a word **ending in a consonant** is **followed by a word that begins with <u>two</u> consonants** (bēt + kbīr), a helping *e* sound is added before the second word. For example:

miš + kbīr → miš‿ekbīr (*not large*)
kamān + mnīḥ → kamān‿ᵉmnīḥ (*also good, good too*)

Explanations 1 and 2 can be summed up neatly in the following table:

il-bēt	id-dars
fi‿l-bēt	fi‿d-dars
il-bēt‿ᵉkbīr	

Don't worry! There's no need for you to try to memorize all this. These are simply explanations that describe what you're seeing (and hearing), so as to satisfy your curiosity. Very soon this will all seem perfectly natural and familiar. Just repeat the examples in the above table... u-bikaffi.

3. The plural form in Arabic

The word walad (*boy*) becomes 'awlād[9] in the plural. In Arabic the plural can assume a large number of different forms: for **every word** you learn you have to memorize the plural form, too.... There's no help for it, but it's not as difficult as it sounds, because certain types of singular and plural tend to go together. In this book we provide the plural form of each word in square brackets. Here is the first list:

bēt	[byūt]	*house*	jār	[jirān]	*neighbor*
dars	[drūs]	*lesson*	walad	['awlād]	*boy*
bint	[banāt]	*girl; daughter*	mαbsūṭ	[mαbsūṭīn][10]	*pleased, feeling well*

4. There isn't / There aren't... I haven't got....

We've seen from the text that *there is / there are, I have got* can be turned into *there isn't / there aren't, I haven't got* by the addition of ma...š:

there is, there are	fīh	*there isn't, there aren't*	ma fī-š
I have got	ᶜindi	*I haven't got*	ma ᶜindī-š

---

9. You may also hear the forms ulād, ewlād (with il-: il-ulād, l-ewlād)

10. The word mαbsūṭ shows us that some words can be made plural by the addition of the suffix -īn rather than by changing the **internal form** of the word.

But when ᶜind means *at* or *at the house of*, it is negated by using miš / muš. For example, compare:

I've got a house	ᶜindi bēt
I haven't got a house	ma ᶜindī-š bēt
Maryam's at my house	Maryam ᶜindi
Maryam's not at my house	Maryam muš ᶜindi
I haven't got [any] money	ma ᶜindī-š mɑṣɑ̄ri
I haven't got the money	il-mɑṣɑ̄ri muš ᶜindi

<the money's not at me / I don't have it here with me>.

Exercises

A. Translate into English:

1. jɑ̄ri ᶜindo ulād
2. 'awlādi ᶜind jɑ̄rak
3. ma ᶜindī-š bint / binet
4. ᶜindi bass walad.
5. bintak ᶜind-ha mɑṣɑ̄ri
6. Yūsef ᶜindo walad
7. il-walad ᶜind Yūsef

B. Complete the sentences:

8. yā Maryam (how are you)?
9. 'ana (not) mɑbsūṭ il-yōm
10. il-jirɑ̄n (at your$^{m\ sing}$ house)?
11. la', il-jirɑ̄n (aren't) ᶜindi
12. šū fīh (on the radio)‿l-yōm?
13. ..il-yōm (there's no) rɑ̄dyo.
14. (Where's) Maryam, u-Yūsef (where's he)?
15. huwwe (at work).
16. Yūsef (has got) ulād.
17. la', Yūsef ma ᶜindō-š (children).

C. Translate into Arabic:

18. Where are your$^{m/f\ sing}$ neighbors?
19. The boy's not at my house.
20. Where's your$^{f\ sing}$ neighbors' house?
21. I haven't got a lesson today.
22. It's not true.
23. I've got money, too <I too, I've got money>.
24. You've$^{m\ sing}$ got a beautiful house, too <you too, you've got a beautiful house>.
25. Where's the money? Haven't you$^{m\ sing}$ got it?
26. No, the money's at home.
27. The neighbors have got the money.
28. I haven't got a radio. There's a radio at the neighbors' [house].

id-dars it-tālet

3

The Third Lesson <the lesson the third>

We've already learned the singular forms of both the personal pronouns ’**a**na, ’**i**nte, ’**i**nti, h**u**wwe, h**i**yye and the possessive pronouns -i, -ak, -ek, -o, -ha. Now it's time to learn their plural forms.

we	’iḥna	our	-na
you^{pl}	’intu	your	-kom^{J} -ku^{G}
they	humme^{J} henne^{G}	their	-hom -hen

Urban speech uses the same word for both masculine and feminine in all these plural forms. Where two different forms are given for the same person, these represent regional variants, e.g.,

bēt-hom = *their house* (in Jerusalemite speech)

bēt-hen = *their house* (in Galilean speech)

In the coming lessons both forms will be given side by side. The Galilee form will appear first, then the Jerusalem form will be given after a double slash. A single slash, on the other hand, will be used to indicate two alternative forms of the same word. For examples see the vocabulary list and text below.

Vocabulary

hāda	this^{m}, this one; that	ta^{c}bān [-īn]	tired, tired out
hāy / hādi	this^{f}; that	mašġūl [-īn]	busy
hadōl	these; those	ṣɑ^{c}b / sɑ^{c}eb	hard, difficult
hal-	this; that; these; those (used before a noun)	mɑbsūṭ min	pleased with
dɑ̄r [dūr] [1]	house	ktīr	very; much, many
min	from, out of	sāknīn	(they) live / living
bɑṭɑ̄le	unemployment	hallaq[2]	now

1. This is another word for *house*, and, like bēt, which you learned in the first lesson, it is also commonly used. However, unlike bēt (which is masculine), dɑ̄r is feminine, and so we say hādi dɑ̄r‿ekbīre (*That's a big house*).

2. hallaq (pronounced halla’), is another word for *now,* used in Jerusalem and understood in Galilee. It's the word used in Lebanon and Syria.

Conversation

– 'iḥna fi bēt-na u-intu fi bēt-ku // bēt-kom.	– We're at our house and you're at your house.
– mīn hadōl?	– Who are they <those>?
– hadōl ulād il-jirān.	– Those are the neighbors' children.
– wēn ulād-ku^{G} 'intu?	– Where are your own children <your-children you>?
– ulād-na bαrrα ma^{c} ulād il-jirān.	– Our children are outside with the neighbors' children.
– il-jirān sāknīn ma^{c} ulād-hom^{J} fi hal-bēt / fi had-dār.	– The neighbors live with their children in that house.
– hāda bēt il-jirān?	– Is that the neighbors' house?
– 'aywa.	– Yes.
– bēt-hom ḥilu ktīr!	– Their house is very nice!
– mαẓbūṭ, henne mαbsūṭīn min hal-bēt.	– Yes it is <True>. They're pleased with the house <from this house>.

– yā Jōrj, šū fī^{h} jdīd?	– What's new, George, <oh George, what is there new>?
– ya ḥabībi, 'ana mašġūl‿^{e}ktīr, u-ta^{c}bān min šuġli.	– Man <my dear>, I'm very busy and tired out from work <from my work>.

– šuġlak ṣɑ^{c}eb?	– Is your work hard?
– ya^{c}ni… miš ṣɑ^{c}eb, bass fīʰ šuġl‿ektīr u-binti kamān ta^{c}bāne mi haš-šuġol.	– Well… not hard, but there's a lot of work, and my daughter's tired out from this work, too.
– 'intu ta^{c}bānīn bass fīʰ šuġol, u-hāda mnīḥ!	– You're tired, but you've got work <there is work> and that's good!
– mɑẓbūṭ, bɑṭɑ̄le ma fi-šš u-hāda 'iši mnīḥ.	– True, there's no unemployment and that's a good thing.

Explanations

1. This (m/f)…, these…; that…, those…

You may already have noticed that the word hal- (which can be used in the masculine or the feminine, the singular or the plural) behaves like the definite article il- when it appears before the "sun letters" mentioned in Lesson 2.

il-+ šuġol = iš-šuġol *the work*

hal- + šuġol = haš-šuġol *this work*

This means that we also say had-dars (*this lesson*), har-rɑ̄dyo *(this radio)*, has-sīnama *(this cinema)* and han-nās *(these people)*.

The word hal- is a shortened form of hāda + il-.

Instead of saying hal-bēt (*this house*), we can say hāda‿l-bēt or il-bēt hāda, and they will all mean the same thing. In the same way, we can say:

hādi‿l-bint / il-bint hādi – instead of hal-bint

hadōl in-nās / in-nās hadōl – instead of han-nās

For our own use, we'll stick to the shortest form, but you'd do well to familiarize yourself with the other forms, too, as you'll hear them used by native speakers.

2. Bint, binet

In both this lesson and the previous one we've come across words that have two different forms: sometimes binet and sometimes bint, sometimes šuġol and sometimes šuġl (as in šuġlak). The "official" forms are bint and šuġl, but the addition of a helping vowel (*e*, *o)* makes them easier to pronounce, especially at the end of a sentence:

wēn il-binet? (*Where's the girl?*) ^{c}indak šuġol? (*Have you got a job?*)

These helping vowels are unnecessary when these words are followed by the endings -i, -ak, -ek, -o. Nor are they used before the definite article il-. This means that we say:

binti	**šu**ġlak	**bi**nt‿il-jir**ā**n	**šu**ġl‿il-b**ē**t
my daughter	*your work*	*the neighbors' daughter*	*housework* *(work-of the house)*

The same form is used before a word that begins with two consonants, such as ktīr, kbīr, mnīḥ – see **Lesson 2**, **Explanations 2** for a description of the helping vowel inserted **before** the following word – because in this case the easiest way to pronounce the combination is:

bint‿ᵉkb**ī**re	not	**bi**nᵉt kb**ī**re
šuġl‿ᵉkt**ī**r	not	**šu**ġᵒl kt**ī**r

■ This can be summarized in a table:

binᵉt	**šu**ġᵒl
binti	**šu**ġlek
bint‿il-jir**ā**n	**šu**ġl‿il-b**ē**t
bint‿ᵉkb**ī**re	**šu**ġl‿ᵉkt**ī**r

As we already suggested in Lesson 2, it's enough just to understand the explanations: there's no need to make an effort to memorize them. Repeat the above table out loud. With time you will find it seems more natural to pronounce these words in accordance with the rules above rather than just "any old how."

3. Stress

If you've been wondering where the stress falls in Arabic words, you'll be glad to know that there are clearly defined rules for this, the first of which is:
If the word contains a long syllable (marked by a line over the vowel), then that syllable is stressed, e.g.,

■ s**ā**ken taᶜb**ā**ne kam**ā**n

Exercises

A. Translate into English:

1. '**a**na taᶜb**ā**n il-y**ō**m.
2. '**i**nte muš taᶜb**ā**n, iš-**šu**ġᵒl h**ō**n muš ṣ**a**ᶜeb.

3. iš-š**u**ġ^{o}l h**ā**da ṣ**α**^{c}b‿^{e}kt**ī**r.
4. h**i**yye ta^{c}b**ā**ne ktīr min š**u**ġ^{o}l-ha.
5. M**a**ryam, ’**i**nti mašġ**ū**le h**a**llaq?
6. l**a**’, ’**a**na miš mašġ**ū**le.
7. w**ē**n sāknīn ewl**ā**dak?
8. h**e**nne sākn**ī**n fi ḥ**ē**fa.
9. f**ī**^{h} š**u**ġ^{e}l fi ḥ**ē**fa?
10. n**a**^{c}am, fī^{h} š**u**ġl‿^{e}kt**ī**r.
11. ’**i**nti, š**u**ġlek ṣ**α**^{ce}b?
12. ’**a**ywa, u-**i**nte š**u**ġlak‿^{e}mn**ī**ḥ.

B. Complete the sentences:

13. h**u**wwe (is pleased) min š**u**ġlak.
14. h**i**yye muš mαbs**ū**ṭα[3] min (your$^{m\ sing}$ work).
15. m**ī**n (that girl)? muš (the manager’s daughter)?
16. f**ī**^{h} h**ō**n (people), h**u**mme jir**ā**nkom?
17. (No), h**u**mme (not) jir**ā**n-na.
18. h**ā**da š**u**ġl (good).
19. il-w**a**lad ([is] outside) ma^{c} il-b**i**n^{e}t.

C. Translate into Arabic:

20. Where do your children live?
21. At their house
22. And those <people>, where do [they] live?
23. Not in that house.
24. Are your (pl) neighbors pleased with my work?
25. Very pleased^{pl}!
26. Aren’t our children outside <Our children aren’t outside>?
    No, they’re at home <in the house>.
27. No, they’re at the neighbors’ house now.
28. My neighbors are pleased with <pleased from> the radio – I’m not <I no>!
29. This lesson’s difficult, I’m tired.
30. OK, that’s enough!

---

3. Why is the feminine ending here *α* not *e*? We’ll explain soon.

id-dars ir-rābe^c

The Fourth Lesson

It's time to discover new ways to use the suffixes -i, -ak, -ek, -o… (i.e., the attached personal pronouns) and the negative suffix **-š,** which "attracts" the stress and moves it to the end of the word:

bidd-[1]	a prefix that expresses *desire, need, wanting*		
bidd-i	*I want*$^{m/f}$	(ma) biddī-š	*I don't want*
bidd-ak	*you*^{m} *want*	(ma) bidd-**ak**-š [2]	*you*^{m} *don't want*
bidd-ek	*you*^{f} *want*	(ma) bidd-kī-š[2]	*you*^{f} *don't want*
bidd-o	*he wants*	(ma) biddō-š	*he doesn't want*

As mentioned in Lesson 2, these personal pronouns can also be attached to prepositions such as ma^c (*with*), minšān / ^{c}ašān (*for, for the sake of*) or mitl / mit^{e}l (*like*). Examples:

ma^{c}i = *with me*, minšānek = *for you*^{f}, mitlo = *like him*

Vocabulary

'ēš?	what (like šu)	waqt / waq^{e}t	time
willa	or	il-ḥaqq[3]	rightness, the truth
'ibn- / 'ib^{e}n	son	ktāb [kutob/kut^{o}b]	book
'ahla u-sahla	welcome[4]	madrase [madāres]	school
maṣāri	money	šāṭer [šāṭrīn]	clever, smart, bright
šāṭra	clever^{f}, smart^{f}	^{e}mbāreḥ / ^{e}mbēreḥ	yesterday
kibrīt	matches	daftar [dafāter]	notebook, exercise book

---

1. You may sometimes also hear baddi, baddak. This pronunciation is common in Lebanon and in northern Galilee along the Lebanese border, in Fassuta, Tarshiha and elsewhere. The form bidd- is used throughout the rest of the country.

2. Note: -ek turns into -kī before the negative suffix -š. The same thing can happen with -ak: some people say bid-kā-š instead of biddak-š (*you don't want*), especially in the Galilee region.

3. Remember that in towns q is not pronounced as an emphatic but as a glottal stop, i.e., the little explosion of air that precedes the pronunciation of a word that begins with a vowel (like *enough*). The word halqēt is pronounced hal…'ēt. So how do you pronounce ḥaqqo (*his right*)? Listen to the recording: ḥa... (the *a* sound breaks off suddenly) -o = ḥa'-'o. How do you pronounce ḥaqq on its own? It's quite easy: you just do the same thing but leave out the -o. Try to pronounce ḥa''e.

Conversation

– m**a**sa‿l-ђ**ē**r.	– Good evening <evening of goodness>!
– m**a**sa‿n-n**ū**r, '**a**hlan u-s**a**hlan![4]	– Good evening <evening of light>, welcome!
– '**a**hlan f**ī**k[5]!	– And the same to you <welcome to you>!
– tf**ɑ**ḍḍɑl[6] f**ū**t, šu b**i**ddak, ya ђ**a**yyi[7]?	– Please come in. What do you want, my friend <my brother>?
– b**i**ddi m**i**nnak '**i**ši zġ**ī**r: fi-šš ᶜ**i**ndi kibr**ī**t fi-l-b**ē**t, f**ī**ʰ ᶜ**i**ndak?	– I need a little something from you. I haven't got any matches at home <there are not at me in the house>; have you got any?
– '**ɑ̄**, maᶜl**ū**m, tf**ɑ**ḍḍɑl! bik**a**ffi? b**i**ddak kam**ā**n '**i**ši t**ā**ni?	– Yes, of course. Here you are <please>! Is that enough? Do you need anything else <also another thing>?
– sal**ā**mtak[6].	– No, thanks <[just] your health>.
– k**ī**f '**i**bnak it-t**ā**ni fi-l-m**a**drase?	– How's your second son [doing] at school?
– ᵉmn**ī**ḥ, il-ḥ**a**mdu-lilla. kam**ā**n il-b**i**nᵉt fi-l-m**a**drase, bass kull h**ā**da b**i**ddo mɑṣ**ɑ̄**ri!	– Fine, thank heavens <praise to God>. The girl's at school, too. But it all costs <all that needs> money!
– minš**ā**n '**ē**š il-mɑṣ**ɑ̄**ri ya ђ**a**yyi[7]?	– What costs money <for what the money>, my friend?
– minš**ā**n il-k**u**tob w-id-daf**ā**ter, kull y**ō**m‿ᵉkt**ā**b‿ᵉjd**ī**d u-kam**ā**n d**a**ftɑr u-kam**ā**n d**a**ftɑr, muš m**u**mken!	– Books <for the books> and exercise books. Every day a new book, another exercise book, then another one <and also an ex.book…> It's impossible!
– bass '**i**nta mɑbs**ū**ṭ min il-m**a**drase u-min l-ewl**ā**d?	– But you're pleased with the school, and with the children?

---

4. The expression '**a**hla u-s**a**hla is less formal than '**a**hlan wa-s**a**hlan, which is borrowed from literary Arabic. It means, literally, *a family and a plain*, i.e., *may our house be like your family home and like a level plain on which you can walk easily and safely*. The word '**a**hᵉl means *family,* and s**a**hᵉl means *plain*, i.e., a safe flat place.

5. The word f**ī**k (you may sometimes also hear b**ī**k) means *in you, at you*ᵐ; explanations later.

6. This will be explained later.

7. This is a Lebanese and Galilean expression.

– ktīr mαbsūṭ min-hom (-hen).	– Very pleased with them.
– ēš biddak 'aktαr min hēk?	– What more do you want <what do you want more than thus>?
– il-ḥaqq maᶜak!	– You're right <rightness is with you>!

– id-dars hāda hayyen[8] willa ṣαᶜeb?	– Is this lesson easy or difficult?
– yaᶜni… muš ṣαᶜb-ᵉktīr.	– Well… not very difficult.
– yaᶜni, hayyen mitl-id-dars il-'awwal?	– You mean it's as easy as the first lesson <it means: easy like the f.l.>?
kull ši[9] biddo waqᵉt.	Everything takes <needs> time.
'inte taᶜbān?	Are your tired?
– il-yōm la', muš mitl-ᵉmbāreḥ.	– Not today <today no>! Not like yesterday.

----

hal-walad šāṭer‿ᵉktīr! fi-šš mitlo fi-l-madrase.	That boy's very bright! There's no-one [else] like him in the school.
– minšān mīn hal-kutob? minšāno willa minšānak?	– Who are these books for < for whom>? For him or for you?
– minšāni.	– For me.

Explanations

1. The word min + attached pronouns, and other matters

The word min becomes minn- before the suffixes -i, -ak, -ek, -o: minni, minnak…. Before the other endings in this paradigm, which begin with a consonant, it doesn't change and remains min- (without doubling of the -n):

min-ha, min-na, min-kom (-ku[G]) min-hom (-hen[G])

---

8. In Galilee you are more likely to hear hwayyen / ᵉhwayyen.

9. This is another form of the word 'iši and it means exactly the same thing.

– The Arabic for *more than* is **'aktɑr min**, and *more than that* is expressed by the Arabic phrase **'aktɑr min hēk** <more than thus>.

– And how do we pronounce min + ktābak *(from your book)*?
min‿ektābak, of course.

2. The definite article (again)

The definite article il- also requires a helping vowel before words that begin with *two consonants*. Sometimes it even "loses its head", drops the i- altogether, and turns into l- / l-e

the book il- + ktāb → il-ektāb / l-ektāb
the big... il- + kbīr → l-ekbīr
the big book = l-ektāb l-ekbīr

When hal- is followed by a word that starts with two consonants a helping vowel is inserted:

this book = hal-ektāb

In **Lesson 2, Explanations 1**, we saw what happens to the definite article before the "sun letters". When a *sun letter* is immediately followed by *another consonant,* you have the choice of two different pronunciations, e.g.,

the little... = il- + zġīr → iz-zġīr / l-ezġīr

– A couple of final comments on the definite article: note that when a noun is followed by an adjective, the definite article is **repeated:**

il-bēt il-ḥilu	*the beautiful house*
il-walad iz-zġīr	*the little boy*

When the definite article is **not** repeated in a phrase like those in the examples above, the phrase turns into a complete sentence with a different meaning:

il- bēt ḥilu	*The house [is] beautiful.*
il-walad‿ezġīr	*The boy [is] small.*

To sum up:

il-bēt ḥilu	the house is beautiful
il-bēt il-ḥilu	the beautiful house
il-bēt‿ekbīr	the house is big
il-bēt l-ekbīr	the big house
hal-walad	this boy
hal-ektāb	this book

3. Words that begin with two consonants – a summary

Words like ktāb, mnīḥ, mbēreḥ:

1) At the beginning of a sentence and **after** a word ending in **a consonant**, these words take an initial ᵉ- to facilitate pronunciation:

– ᵉmnīḥ!	min‿ᵉktābo	mitl‿ᵉmbēreḥ
– *Well!*	*from his book*	*like yesterday*

2) When these words appear **after a vowel** (after a word ending in a vowel) this ᵉ- is unnecessary.

bēt-na kbīr	bēt-na fi ḥēfa kbīr	šuġlo mnīḥ
our house is big	*our house in Haifa is big*	*his work is good*

4. What? = šū? ’ēš ?

Normally it doesn't matter which of these two words you use, as they both mean the same thing. However**, after a preposition**, the word ’ēš is much more usual:

’inte mαbsūṭ min ’ēš?	ᶜala ’ēš ?	minšān ’ēš ?
What are you pleased about?	*on what?*	*What for?*

Take care to pronounce the glottal stop ’ clearly.
Don't say *minesh* or *minshanesh* – say *minshān... ’ēsh.*

Exercises

A. Translate into English:

1. hal-ᵉktāb‿ᵉmnīḥ
2. wēn il-bēt ij-jdīd (il-bēt l-ᵉjdīd)?
3. bintak bid(d)-ha [10] mαṣᾱri.
4. bid(d)nā-š dafāter, kull wāḥed ᶜindo daftαr, bikaffi.
   bidna[10] bass kutob.
5. ᶜind-kom (-ku) kutob?
6. la’, ma ᶜind-na-š (ᶜin-nā-š[10]).

B. Complete the sentences (add a helping vowel where necessary):

Examples:

wēn daftαrak? *but* wēn ktābak → wēn‿ᵉktābak?
minšān darsi *but* minšān drūsi → minšān‿ᵉdrūsi

7. binti kbīre.
8. binto kamān kbīre.
9. biddi ktāb.
10. biddi kamān ktāb.
11. šuġli mnīḥ.
12. mαẓbūṭ, šuġlak mnīḥ.
13. hāda ktīr!
14. la', hāda muš ktīr.

C. Translate into Arabic:

– When you write this exercise, underline the vowel of the stressed syllable, or indicate it with the sign <.

< <
biddo / biddō-š

15. He lives with his son in the new house.
16. What does she need (want) money for <for what she needs money>?
17. Who's right? <with whom is the rightness> – I'm right!
18. I'm not pleased with you^{m} .
19. That boy's got <has got> books and exercise books, and that's enough for school <for the school>.
20. Does your$^{m\ sing}$ daughter want another (**kamān**) book? No, she doesn't <want>.
21. Do you^{pl} want work or money?
22. We don't want money, we want work![10]
23. There's a big school here.
24. You've $^{m\ sing}$ got more money than me <you've got money more than me>.
25. This is for me.
26. Yes, this is for you $^{f\ sing}$.
27. He's got more money than all the neighbors.
28. I don't have time now.
29. I've only got a little book.
30. I'm tired ^{m}! – From what <tired from what>?

---

10. **bidd-ha, bidd-na, ᶜind-na** – Don't put too much effort into trying to pronounce the doubled consonants here, as what people actually say is **bid-ha, bidna, ᶜin-na.**

In Arabic we say *one and twenty, two and twenty, three and twenty....*, like the nursery rhyme: "Four and twenty blackbirds baked in a pie."

id-dars il-ḫāmes

5

The Fifth Lesson

Today we’re going to tackle the verb. First of all we’ll explore it through the texts below, then we’ll draw conclusions about it in the **Explanations.**

Vocabulary

’**u**ḫt	sister	’**imm** (also ’**u**mm)	mother
l**ā**zem	must <necessary>	k**u**rsi [kɑr**ɑ̄**si] [1]	chair
muš l**ā**zem	must not < not necessary>	taᶜ**ā**l	come^{m}!
baᶜd**ē**n	afterwards, later	jar**ī**de [jar**ɑ̄**yed]	newspaper
bal**ā**š(-ma)	don’t…! (used in negative commands)		
ᶜaš**ā**n	for, because of; in order to	la-h**ō**n	(to) here
mɑr**ī**ḍ$^{m\ sing}$	ill, sick, patient	hun**ā**k	there
mɑr**ī**ḍɑ$^{f\ sing}$	ill, sick, patient	kw**a**yyes	good, well
dokt**ō**r	doctor	šw**a**yy	a little

Conversation

– ya Y**ū**sef, taᶜ**ā**l la-h**ō**n!	– Yusef, come here <to here>!
– š**ū** fī^{h}, ya b**ɑ̄**bɑ?	– What is it, Dad <oh Dad>?
– r**ū**ḥ, j**ī**b id-dokt**ō**r minš**ā**n ’**u**ḫtak.	– Go and get <bring> the doctor for your sister.
– š**ū**? h**i**yye mɑr**ī**ḍɑ ?	– What, is she ill?
– l**a**’, muš mɑr**ī**ḍɑ, bass	– No, not ill, just not
muš mabs**ū**ṭɑ šw**a**yy.	feeling well.
r**ū**ḥ qaw**ɑ̄**m la-ᶜ**i**nd id-dokt**ō**r,	Go to the doctor’s straight away
q**ū**l la-d-dokt**ō**r:	[and] tell the doctor,
taᶜ**ā**l la-ᶜ**i**ndna (ᶜ**i**n-na),	“Come to our house,
M**a**ryam m**u**š mabs**ū**ṭɑ.	Maryam’s not feeling well.”
– ṭ**ɑ**yyeb.	– OK.

– w**ē**n id-dokt**ō**r?	– Where’s the doctor?
– hayy**ā**h^{G} / h**a**yyo^{J}.	– Here he is.[2]

1. This word is feminine in Galilee, masculine in Jerusalem (and elsewhere).
2. This will be explained on page 69.

– tfaḍḍal[3] yā sayyed Elyās, fūt!	– Please come in, Mr. Elias.
kīf ḥālak?	How are you <how is your condition>?
– il-ḥamdilla, kīf ḥālak 'inte?	– Thank God. How's yourself,
u-kīf ḥāl bintak?	and how's your daughter?
– yaᶜni, taᶜāl šūf 'inta	– So-so. Come and see for yourself
u-qul-li kīf ḥāl-ha.	<come, see, you> and tell me how she is.
– wēn-ha?	– Where is she?
– hōn, fi-l-'ōḍa.	– Here, in her room <in the room>.
tfaḍḍal fūt!	Please come in!

Don't worry, Maryam will get better soon, but the vocabulary we've learned so far is insufficient to tell you about it.

– yā Maryam, taᶜāli! rūḥi jībi	– Maryam, come here! [4]
kursi minšān 'immek.	Go and get a chair for your mother.
– wēn il-jarīde?	– Where's the newspaper?
ᶜa-l-kursi (ᶜala‿l-kursi)?	On the chair?
– la', yimken ᶜa-ṭ-ṭāwle.	– No. It may be on the table <it's possible on the table>.
– la ᶜa-l-kursi wala ᶜa-ṭ-ṭāwle.	– [It's] neither on the chair nor on the table.[5]
– ma ᶜalēš (ma ᶜalešš).	– Never mind.[6]
(Yusef:)	
– biddak ajīb jarīde	– Do you want me to get a newspaper
min ᶜind il-jirān?	from the neighbors' <from at the n.>?
– 'aywa, hāy fikra kwayyse.	– Yes, that's a good idea.
– biddi arūḥ 'issa / halqēt	– I'll go <I want that I go> now [and]
'ajib-lak hal-jarīde.	get you the paper <that I bring you this p.>.
– la', balāš-ma trūḥ 'issa,	– No, don't go now.
bᵉtrūḥ baᶜdēn.	Go later <you will go later>.

---

3. You've been invited to do something (to sit down, have a drink, take something, join in something) – what do you reply? We won't tell you just yet.
4. Note the feminine ending *-i* of the verb.
5. To say *neither..... nor*, we don't use muš / miš, but la… wa-la… (or la… wa-la...) instead.
6. This will be explained later.

– ᵉmbala⁷, barūḥ 'issa. — No, I'll go now.

(biddo irūḥ 'issa ᶜašān (He wants to go now because
biddo išūf ewlād il-jirᾱn) he wants to see the neighbors' children.)

– ṭɑyyeb, rūḥ, bass qawᾱm! — Fine, go, but quickly!

'ana kamān biddi arūḥ ᶜa-l-madrase!

Explanations

1. The verb

Let's see what new things we've learned today:

rūḥ	goᵐ!	jīb	bringᵐ
a-rūḥ ('a-)	that I go	a-jīb ('a-)	that I bring
ba-rūḥ	I go / I'll go	ba-jīb	I bring / I'll bring
rūḥ	goᵐ!	jībi	bringᶠ
t-rūḥ / ᵉt-rūḥ	that youᵐ go	t-jībi / ᵉt-jībi	that youᶠ bring
bᵉt-rūḥ	youᵐ go / you'll go	bᵉt-jībi	youᶠ bring / you'll bring

Here, for the first time, we are meeting three different tenses and moods of the verb: the imperative, the subjunctive and the present-future. English speakers sometimes find it hard to understand exactly what the "subjunctive mood" is. At this point we'll make do with a partial explanation:

---

7. **mbala (ᵉmbala)** means *yes it is / yes I will!*, etc., or *no, on the contrary*, and it is used in response to a negative sentence (in this case: *don't go now....*) in order to correct or contradict what has just been said, e.g.,

– biddō-š irūḥ?   – Doesn't he want to go?
– ᵉmbala !   – Yes, he does!

A verb in the **subjunctive** follows **lāzem** ([*it is*] *necessary that*) and verbs that express a desire, a wish or an intention, such as **biddi** (*I want*).

biddi ašūf	*I want to see* <I want that I see>
biddak‿et-šūf	*You*$^{\text{m sing}}$ *want to see* <you want that you see>
lāzem 'a-jīb	*I must bring…* < [I] must that I bring>

Note: English, too, has a subjunctive mood, though today it is not always used. You can hear it in sentences like "I insist that he leave" (not "that he leaves").

– ajīb, t-jīb, i-šūf are all verbs in the subjunctive.

– To form the present-future tense we simply add the prefix b- to the verb in the subjunctive: b-ajīb, b-^{e}tjīb, b-išūf.

We'll learn the various uses of the present-future tense gradually as we progress, and we'll come back a number of times to discuss the issue of tenses and verbal moods.

2. And what if she sees, brings, etc?

First of all, let's sum things up:

ajīb	*that I bring*	bajīb	*I bring / I'll bring*
tjīb	*that you*^{m} *bring*	b^{e}tjīb	*you*^{m} *bring / you'll bring*
tjībi	*that you*^{f} *bring*	b^{e}tjībi	*you*^{f} *bring / you'll bring*
ijīb	*that he bring*	bijīb	*he brings / he'll bring*

And let's add:

tjīb	*that she bring*	b^{e}t-jīb	*she brings / she'll bring*

Worth noting: The third person feminine singular form (*she*) is identical with the second person masculine form (*you*^{m}) in both the subjunctive and the present-future. We'll come back to this later.

3. Bring to, say to

In expressions such as *bring to…, say to… / tell (somebody)…*, the Arabic preposition l- / la is used:

id-doktōr	*the doctor*
qūl la-d-doktōr!	*Tell the doctor!*
'immak	*your mother*
qūl la-'immak	*Tell your mother!*

And before the suffixes -i, -ak, -o, etc.,

q**u**l-li – baq**u**l-lak	*Tell me! – I'll tell you*[m]
baj**i**b-lak	*I'll bring you* <to you>...
b**i**ddi aq**u**l-lak	*I want to say to you / to tell you*
l**ā**zem aq**u**l-lek	*I must tell you*[f]

Note:

When -li, -lak, etc. are added to a verb that ends in a consonant, the combination of the **two consonants** (aqul-lak, jib-li) causes the long vowel that precedes them to become short **-ū-** → **-u-**, **-ī-** → **-i-** :

■ baq**ū**l → baq**u**l-lak
(long) (short)
bij**ī**b → bij**i**b-lak

4. Go to, travel to

The preposition l- is used before certain specific words to indicate movement towards:

'**i**nte ᶜ**i**ndo	*You're at his house* <you're at him / by him>
r**ū**ḥ la-ᶜ**i**ndo	*Go to his house* <go to at him / by him>!
h**u**wwe hun**ā**k	*He's there*
r**ū**ḥ la-hun**ā**k!	*Go there* <go to there>!

In most cases, however, **before a noun, movement from place to place** is indicated by the preposition ᶜ**a**la / ᶜala (or just ᶜa-) whose basic meaning is *on*. And so, in order to say *go to* (before a noun), we'll use ᶜala:

■	h**u**wwe s**ā**ken fi ḥ**ē**fa	*He lives in Haifa.*
	bir**ū**ḥ ᶜala ḥ**ē**fa	*He goes to Haifa.*

Or, for a change:

■	h**u**mme sākn**ī**n fi n**ā**bles	*They live in Nablus.*
	bir**ū**ḥu ᶜala r**ī**ḥa	*They travel to Jericho.*
	'**i**nta s**ā**ken fi‿l-ђal**ī**l?	*Do you live in Hebron?*
	b**i**ddi ar**ū**ḥ ᶜa-l-ђal**ī**l	*I want to go to Hebron.*
	l-ewl**ā**d fi‿l-m**a**drase	*The children are at school.*
	r**ū**ḥ ᶜa-l-m**a**drase	*Go to school / the school!*
	'**i**mmak fi‿l-b**ē**t	*Your mother's at home / in the house.*
	f**ū**t ᶜa-l-b**ē**t	*Go* <enter> *into the house!*

Exercises

A. Translate into English:

1. ya Maryam, lāzem‿tjībi kursi.
2. biddak ajīb kamān kursi?
3. la', muš lāzem!
4. ta^{c}āl la-^{c}in(d)-na ma^c 'uђtak.
5. ^{c}indo šuġl‿^{e}mnīḥ u-kull yōm bijīb mαṣᾱri ^{c}a-l-bēt.
6. biddek‿trūḥi / ma bid(d)kī-š‿^{e}trūḥi?
7. embala! biddi arūḥ ma^{c}o.
8. 'ana kamān biddi ajīb mαṣᾱri la-'immi.

B. Complete:

* = necessity, intention: use the subjunctive (without the prefix b-)

** = a fact in the present or future: use the present-future (with the prefix b-)

9. He's got to get <[it is] necessary that he bring> the doctor.
   lāzem * id-doktōr.
10. Now he gets / he'll get (bring) the paper.
   'issa ** il-jarīde.
11. He's got to see the school <[it is necessary that] he see>.
   lāzem * il-madrase.
12. He wants to go to the neighbors' <to by the neighbors>.
   biddo * la-^{c}ind il-jirᾱn.

13. He'll go to school tomorrow <tomorrow he'll go to the school>
 bukra ** ^{c}a-l-**madrase.**
14. Why do you want to go there <why do you want that you go to there>?
 lēš[8] **biddak‿** * **la-hunāk?**
15. Do you^{f} want to see your daughter?
 biddek‿ * **bintek?**
16. You'll see your daughter tomorrow <tomorrow you'll see…>.
 bukrɑ[9] ** **bintek.**

C. Translate into Arabic:

17. Yusef, go to your mother / your mother's!
 – Come into the house, Mum (**mɑ̄ mɑ**) <oh Mum, enter into…..>.
18. I've got to go to school now. Tomorrow I'll go to school.
19. Do you $^{\text{m sing}}$ want to see my daughter? She's not at home.
20. Maryam, do you want to go to school with us (**ma^{c}na**) <with us to the school>?
 – No, I'll go later.
21. Why? – Because (**li'anno**) I'm busy.
22. Hey boy, you mustn't go into the neighbors' house <it mustn't [be] that you enter into the house of the neighbors>.
23. He's right! (see page 20).
24. I don't want to go to school <to the school>. I want to go to Haifa.
25. OK, go$^{\text{m sing}}$ to Haifa with your sister <with your sister to Haifa> and bring me back a newspaper <bring me a newspaper from there>.
26. He mustn't see <it must not that he see> that on the table.

And the final exercise:

Read out loud: "I want to see, you want to see……"

■ **biddi ašūf – biddak‿tšūf – biddek‿tšūfi – biddo išūf**
biddī-š ašūf – biddak-š‿etšūf – bid(d)kī-š‿etšūfi – biddō-š‿išūf

If you were chuffing away like a steam engine when you read the second line, try repeating the exercise with the verb **fūt**, just for a change: **biddi afūt** or with the verb **jīb**: **biddī-š ajīb.**

---

8. No problem understanding this: l- + 'ēš → **lēš** (*for what* = *why*).
9. This is a new word for us. Now we can say: **embēreḥ, il-yōm u-bukrɑ.**

id-dars is-sādes

6

The Sixth Lesson

Today we're going to complete the paradigm of the verb in the imperative and the present-future by adding the plural forms:

■ fūtu	Come in! / Go in!
t-fūtu	that you go in (intention, command)
lāzem‿etfūtu	You must go in
bid(d)kom‿etfūtu[1]	Do you want to go in?
'issa / halqēt bitfūtu	You'll come / go in now.
lāzem‿ifūtu	They must come / go in.
halqēt / hallaq bifūtu	They'll come / go in now.

The prefix for *I* (1st person singular) is a- (as we saw in the previous lesson), while for *we* (1st person plural) it is n-:

lāzem‿en-jīb	We must bring
bid(d)na‿n-jīb (= bidna‿njīb)	We want to bring / We're going to bring
b-enjīb // m-enjīb G	We bring[2]

Lāzem ifūtu !
'issa bifūtu

1. In Galilee people say: bid-ku‿tfūtu.
2 In Galilee, Lebanon and Syria, people add m-e instead of b-e before n-.

Vocabulary

il-quds (q̈uds)	Jerusalem	'ēmta (winta[G])	when?
in-nɑ̄ṣre	Nazareth	bukrɑ	tomorrow [4]
^{c}amm	paternal uncle	ba^{c}d / ba^{ce}d	after
'aḥsan	better	zūr	visit!
qab^{e}l	before	i-zūr	that he visit
qab^{e}l-ma	before + verb	kūn	be!
li'anno (la'inno)	because	i-kūn	that he be
ḥatta / ^{c}ašān	so that	mūt!	die![5]
ђetyɑ̄r [3]	old [man]	i-mūt	that he die
[ђetyɑ̄riyye]		dāyman	always

Conversation

– ya Mūsa, 'ēmta biddak‿^{e}trūḥ ^{c}a-l-quds? – lēš?	– Musa, when do you want to go to Jerusalem? – Why?
– li'anno biddi arūḥ ma^{c}ak.	– Because I want to go with you.
– 'ahlan wa-sahlan[6] ('ahla u-sahla)! barūḥ bukrɑ 'in šɑllɑ[7]. biddi ašūf ^{c}ammi hunāk.	– You're welcome [to come with me]. I'm going tomorrow, God willing. I want to see my uncle there.
– ^{c}ammak sāken fi-l-quds?	– Does your uncle live in Jerusalem?
– 'ɑ̄, min zamān. dāyman biqul-li: lāzem‿^{e}tzūr ^{c}ammak il-ђetyɑ̄r qab^{e}l-ma‿imūt.	– Yes, for a long time [now]. He always tells me: You've got to visit your old uncle before he dies

3. Some people pronounce this word ^{e}ђtyɑ̄r, and, after the definite article il-, l-^{e}ђtyɑ̄r, like l-^{e}ktāb (see **Lesson 4**, **Explanations 2**).

4. bukrɑ does not always mean *tomorrow* in the narrow sense of the English word; rather, it means *not today*. In our text, however, bukrɑ often actually does mean *tomorrow* (God willing…).

5. Obviously, this form is rarely used. It is, however, the "basic form" of the verb.

6. When one person expresses a request or intention that depends on the agreement of another, this formula is used to convey an affirmative response.

7. Literally: *if God wants.* In literary Arabic: 'in šɑ̄' 'ɑllɑ̄h. In colloquial Arabic *God* (Allah) is pronounced 'ɑllɑ. In everyday speech in inšɑllɑ usually means *I hope / Let's hope.*

– yih! qaddēš ^{c}umro?	– Oh! How old is he <how-much his age>?
– tis^{c}īn[8] sane // sine.	– Ninety <ninety years>.
– ya salām! miš qalīl[9]!	– Wow <oh peace>! That's a good age <not a little>.
^{e}nšalla[10] ma bimut-š	Let's hope <if God wills> he won't die
qab^{e}l-ma‿trūḥ ^{c}a-l-quds.	before you go to Jerusalem!
– ^{c}ašān hēk biddi arūḥ bukra.	– That's why <because of thus> I want to go tomorrow.
– ṭayyeb, bukra m^{e}nrūḥ sawa.	– OK, tomorrow we'll go together.

(They went, and found the uncle in excellent health)

– ta^{c}āl qawām, lāzem‿^{e}nrūḥ	– Come quickly, we've got to go <it must that we go>
^{c}a-l-maḥaṭṭa.	to the bus stop.
– fīh bāṣ[11] ba^{c}d‿^{e}šwayy.	There's a bus soon <after a bit>.
lāzem‿^{e}nkūn fi ḥēfa	We've got to be in Haifa
qabl‿is-sē^{c}a tis^{c}a,	before nine o'clock <before the hour nine>,
u-ba^{c}dēn barūḥ ^{c}a-n-nāṣre (-ra)	and afterwards I'll go to Nazareth.
– qaddēš is-sē^{c}a hallaq?	– What time is it <how much is the hour> now?
– sab^{c}a tamām.	– Seven [o'clock] precisely.
– ^{c}indna waq^{e}t,[12]	– We've got time.
bidna bass	It takes only <we want only>
nuṣṣ sē^{c}a min hōn la-ḥēfa.	half an hour from here to Haifa
– ma^{c}alešš. 'aḥsan‿^{e}nrūḥ 'issa	– It doesn't matter. We should go <better we go> now

---

8. Note that the noun being counted here (sane) appears in the singular (in Arabic we say *ninety year*, not *ninety years*). We'll learn the rules for counting soon.

9. qalīl = *a little, not a lot. That's very little* or *That's not very much at all* = hāda qalīl‿^{e}ktīr ...

10. See footnote 7.

11. This word is, of course, borrowed from English, but its plural form is very Arabic: [bāṣāt]. See below **Explanations 1**, Pronunciation problems.

12. It's hard to say waqt (wa't), and so we add an *e* sound (as in bint→ bin^{e}t) and say waq^{e}t instead. However, waqt + il = waqt‿il, e.g., waqt‿id-dars (*during the lesson*). The same thing happens in the expression waqt‿^{e}ktīr (*a long time, a lot of time*) – see p.15 **Explanations 2**.

ḥatta‿nšūf ’iza[13] **fīh bāṣ tāni.**	so that we can see if there’s another bus.
– **ṭayyeb, bidna‿nrūḥ ’issa**	– OK, let’s go <we’ll go> now,
ḥatta‿tkūn mabsūṭ.	to please you <so that you’ll be pleased>.

Now we can summarize the subjunctive and present-future verbal forms in the following tables:

To bring

	subj	pres-fut		subj	pres-fut
I	**a-jīb**	**b -a-jīb**	*we*	**n-jīb**	**b-enjīb / m-enjīb** ^{G}
you $^{m\ sing}$	**t-jīb***	**b-et-jīb***	*you* $^{m/f\ pl}$	**t-jību**	**b-et-jību**
you $^{f\ sing}$	**t-jībi**	**b-et-jībi**			
he	**i-jīb**	**b -i-jīb**	*they* $^{m/f\ pl}$	**i-jību**	**b-i-jību**
she	**t-jīb***	**b-et-jīb***			

		≠			
I	a-	≠	n-	*we*	If you find this table puzzling, just ignore it!
you $^{m\ sing}$	→ t-		t- – u	*you*	
you $^{f\ sing}$	t-– i				
he	i-		i- –u	*they*	
she	→ t-				

---

* Yes, the forms for *you* $^{m\ sing}$ and *she* are identical, though the context generally helps to show which is meant; for example:

■ **barūḥ maᶜak la-ᶜind ’immak** *I’ll go with you to your mother’s [house],*
ḥatta‿tkūn mabsūṭ – *to please you* <so that you’ll be pleased ^{m}>.
ḥatta‿tkūn mabsūṭa – *to please her* <so that she’ll be pleased ^{f}>

However, things are not always quite so clear-cut, and you may well hear conversations like the following:

---

13. As in English, **’iza** is used both in conditional sentences (*if you want* =**’iza biddak**) and to express a question after a verb: *I’ll see if there’s [any] money* = **biddi ašūf ’iza fīh maṣāri**.

(...) *I'll phone to-morrow morning*

ḥatta‿tk**ū**n fi-l-b**ē**t. *so that you'll / she'll be at home.*

– m**ī**n? h**i**yye (w**i**lla '**a**na)? – *Who? Her (or me)?*

Or the speaker may take care to be more explicit:

ḥatta '**inte**‿tk**ū**n fi-l-b**ē**t. *so that **you**'ll be at home.*

Explanations

1. Pronunciation problems

1) First of all, there is no need to pronounce every doubled consonant that is not followed by a vowel exactly as written, as in such cases the doubling is not always heard. For example, you will often hear b**i**dd-na, b**i**ddkom pronounced as b**i**dna, b**i**dkom. A similar phenomenon can be observed in the word ᶜ**i**ndna: the d is sometimes dropped, and you will hear ᶜ**i**n-na instead.

2) Why does the word bim**ū**t (with a long *oo* sound) become bim**u**t-š (with a short *u* sound) when the negative suffix -š is added? Perhaps you have already guessed. As in the case of q**ū**l → q**u**l-li, here, too, the vowels **ī** / **ū** shortens when -š is added: bij**ī**b → bij**i**b-š. Nonetheless, you will sometimes hear people say ma bij**ī**b-š (*he doesn't bring*).

3) Note the difference in pronunciation between the words b**ā**ṣ and b**a**ss (*bus* and *only; enough! / stop!*)

b**ā**ṣ is pronounced with a long "dark" *aah* sound produced at the back of the mouth (rather like the *aah* sound we make when we yawn). ṣ is like *s* in English, but "fuller" and less sibilant.

b**a**ss is pronounced with a short "open" *a* (produced further forward in the mouth than the *aah* described above); s is just like the English *s*, but as it is doubled here you have to hold it for twice the usual length of time. Perhaps the following illustration will help: b**āāā**ṣ (b**ɑ**ṣ) ≠ b**a**ssss.

2. The subjunctive

The subjunctive mood, which we used after b**i**ddi and l**ā**zem, is also used after '**a**ḥsan, q**a**bᵉl-ma, **ḥ**atta and ᶜaš**ā**n / ᶜala-š**ā**n (in the sense of *in order to / so that*).

'**a**ḥsan‿ᵉtr**ū**ḥ	q**a**bᵉl-ma‿tr**ū**ḥ	**ḥ**atta‿tr**ū**ḥ
You'd better go	*before you go*	*so that you go*

<[it's] better [that] you go>

3. The two different meanings of ᶜašān before a verb

You will most probably already have noticed that the word ᶜašān (ᶜala-šān) has two meanings:
– *in order to / so that*, followed by a verb in the subjunctive.
– *because*, followed by a verb in the appropriate tense (past or present-future).

ᶜašān irūḥ maᶜak	*so that he'll go with you* (intention)
ᶜašān birūḥ ᶜa-l-madrase	*because he goes to school* (fact)

4. Jerusalem

In Arabic Jerusalem is referred to as "The Holy [City]," i.e., il-quds, pronounced with either a glottal stop (') or with a throaty back *q* sound, as in literary Arabic. You will hear people say il-q̈uds / il-quds ('uds) / il-qodᵉs.

5. The various meanings of kamān

We have already seen that kamān means *also / too / as well* and *another*

– When kamān means *also* or *too*, it is usually placed **after** the word it refers to, as in English:

'ana kamān	*I, too / me too*
il-yōm kamān	*today also / today too*

– When kamān means *more* or *another* (in the sense of "an additional"), it is usually placed **before** the word it refers to:

kamān!	*more!*
kamān wāḥad	*another one* <an additional one>
kamān mαrrα	*again* <an additional time>
kamān‿ᵉktāb	*another* <an additional> *book*

Note that kamān cannot always be used to translate the English word *another*. If you want to say *another one* in the sense of *a different one*, you can’t use kamān. This will be explained on page 67, **Explanations 3**.

Exercises

A. Translate into English:

1. fūt ’inte, ’ana bafūt baᶜdēn.
2. il-walad ma biddō-š ifūt.
3. ᵉmbala, biddo‿ifūt maᶜ ’uḫto.
4. hallaq birūḥ la-ᶜind ᶜammo ḫalīl. biddak‿ᵉtrūḥ ’inte kamān?
5. la’, hallaq ’ana mašġūl / mašġūle, barūḥ bukra.
6. l-ᵉwlād bid(d)hom irūḥu ᶜa-s-sīnama.
7. ’iza bitrūḥ ’inte, ’ana barūḥ maᶜak.

B. Complete the sentences

(Replace the English words with the appropriate expression in Arabic):

8. ’iza bišūf hāda, bikūn mɑbsūṭ,
   u-’inti, ’iza (you^{f} see) hāda, (you’ll be pleased).
9. bukrɑ l-ᵉwlād bikūnu mɑbsūṭīn li’anno ma-fī-š madrase.
   (I, too) bakūn mɑbsūṭ (because there’s no lesson).
10. Yūsef sāken fi-n-Nɑ̄ṣre, u-Maryam (lives in Jerusalem).
11. biddi arūḥ ᶜa-n-Nɑ̄ṣre u-hiyye bid-ha (to go to Jerusalem).
12. bukrɑ barūḥ kamān mɑrrɑ. – ṭɑyyeb jib-li (another one).
13. bukra lāzem‿ᵉnrūḥ ᶜa-l-madrase, (and today as well)!

C. Translate into Arabic:

14. You^{m} don’t have to go <it is not necessary that you go> now. You’ll go tomorrow.
15. We’ve got to leave here <it is necessary [that] we go from here> to please him <so that [he] will be pleased>.
16. You^{m} should go and see him now <better you go to at him (….)> because he’s ill.
17. Bring^{m} the radio here so that the neighbors don’t get upset <so that the neighbors will be pleased>.
18. If you^{m} bring the radio, they’ll be pleased.
19. You^{m} mustn’t bring <it must not be [that] you bring> the book here.

20. He doesn’t want to go to Jerusalem <on Jerusalem>, he wants to go with us to Haifa.
21. Do you^{m} want to go to Nazareth?
22. Yes. My son is at school <in the school> in Nazareth.
23. If he goes in, I’ll go in with him.

This evening, before you go to bed, repeat the following forms out loud:

biddi ar**ū**ḥ	(ma) bidd**ī**-š arūḥ
biddak‿^{e}tr**ū**ḥ	(ma) bidd**a**k-š‿^{e}truḥ
biddek‿^{e}tr**ū**ḥi	(ma) bidk**ī**-š‿^{e}tr**ū**ḥi
biddo ir**ū**ḥ	(ma) bidd**ō**-š‿ir**ū**ḥ
bidna‿^{e}nr**ū**h	(ma) bidn**ā**-š‿^{e}nr**ū**ḥ
bidkom‿^{e}tr**ū**ḥu	(ma) bidk**o**m-š‿^{e}tr**ū**ḥu
bidku‿tr**ū**ḥu^{G}	(ma) bidk**u**š‿^{e}tr**ū**ḥu^{G}
bidhom‿ir**ū**ḥu	(ma) bidh**o**m-š‿ir**ū**ḥu
bidhen‿ir**ū**ḥu^{G}	(ma) bidh**e**n(n^{e})š ir**ū**ḥu^{G}

You may have noticed that a is not always preceded by a glottal stop (’). This is because the glottal stop weakens and vanishes when it follows a vowel, and so we have written [**bi**ddi ’ar**ū**ḥ →] **bi**ddi ar**ū**ḥ and [u-’i**ḥ**na→] u-**iḥ**na, etc. More about this at the end of this book, p.110.

id-dars is-sābeᶜ —————————————————————————7

The Seventh Lesson

Let's extend our possibilities further: we have seen that -ak, -ek, -o, -na, etc., are used:

After a preposition: ᶜind-ak, minšān-o, maᶜ-na

After a noun (as a possessive pronoun): 'ibn-ak, bint-o, jirān-kom

These suffixes can also be used to express the direct object of a verb (*you, him, us, them*). Here are a few examples

bazūr-ak	*I visit you*
bizūr-na	*He visits us*
lāzem‿etjīb-o	*You must bring him / it*
lāzem‿etjīb-ha	*You must bring her / it*
bidna‿nzūr-hom//-hen	*We want to visit them*

The suffixes used to express a direct object in cases like these have exactly the same form as the attached pronouns we learned earlier – with one exception!

In the 1ˢᵗ person singular we don't say bizūr-i but, instead, bizūr-ni (*he visits me*).

jār-ak bizūr-ak	*Your neighbor visits you*
jār-i bizūr-ni	*My neighbor visits me*

fi ḥēfa   fi-l-quds

Vocabulary

'**a**b ('**a**bb)	father	'**a**ђ ('**a**ђђ) ['**i**ђwe]	brother
'**a**bu	father-of	'**a**ђu	brother-of
'ab**ū**y	my father[1]	'aђ**ū**y	my brother
q**ū**l	tell!	'**u**ђt [ђaw**ā**t]	sister
z**ī**ḥ	move!	š**a**ms [f]	sun
b**ā**b	door	l**ō**n ['alw**ā**n]	color, shade
z**a**lame	man, guy	'**i**lli / illi	that, which, who, whom
busukl**ē**t [2]	bicycle	b**α**rrα	outside, outdoors
'inn / '**i**nno[3]	that (conjunction)	j**u**wwa	inside, indoors
'**a**zrαq	blue	muђt**ᾱ**r [maђat**ī**r]	village headman, *mukhtar*
'**a**ḥmαr	red	j**a**mb / ḥ**a**dd	next to, beside
'**a**byαḍ	white	m**α**ṭbαђ	kitchen
'**a**yya / '**a**yy	which? (used before a noun)		
'**a**yya w**ā**ḥad [4]	which one	muft**ā**ḥ [maf**ā**t**ī**ḥ]	key

Conversation

– il-muђt**ᾱ**r b**i**ddo iš**ū**fak.	– The *mukhtar* wants to see you.
– u-**a**na kam**ā**n b**i**ddi aš**ū**fo.	– And I want to see him, too.
– '**i**za h**ē**k, l**ā**zem‿ᵉtz**ū**ro.	– If so <if thus>, you'll have to pay him a visit <it is necessary that you visit him>.
– '**a**ḥsan inno[3] <u>h**ū**</u> iz**ū**r-ni	– It would be better if **he** came to see me <better that he visit me>!
d**ā**yman biq**ū**l: b**i**ddi az**ū**rkom fi b**ē**t-kom l-ᵉjd**ī**d.	He's always saying "I want to visit you in your new house."
– h**ē**k‿ᵉmn**ī**ḥ: bir**ū**ḥ laᶜ**i**nd in-n**ā**s u-biz**ū**r-hom [fi by**ū**t-hom].	– Good idea <thus [is] good>! He'll go to [see] people, and visit them [in their homes].
– h**ē**k l**ā**zem!	– That's the way it should be <thus [it is] necessary>.

----

1. This will be explained later.
2. In Jerusalem you'll hear baskal**ē**t. In Galilee busukl**ē**t is generally feminine.
3. Used after a verb (*He says that...*), or in expressions like *It's best that....*, *It's important that...* See the **Conversation** and **Explanations 3**.
4. Note that the Arabic expression here is exactly the same as the English.

– yā Nāṣer!	– Nasser!
– šū fīʰ ya māma?	– What is it, Mum <what is there>?
– šū lōn l-ᵉktāb illi ᶜa-ṭ-ṭāwle?	– What color is the book that's on the table? <what [is] color-of the book…>?
–'ayya ktāb biddek? fīʰ wāḥad 'aḥmar u-fīʰ wāḥad 'azraq. 'ayya wāḥad biddek?	– Which book do you want? There's a red one <one red> and there's a blue one. Which one do you want?
– miš hadōl; l-ᵉktāb illi ḥadd id-dafāter (jamb id-dafāter). lōno 'abyaḍ, muš hēk? jību u-zīḥ il-burdāy ᶜan iš-šubbāk ᶜašān‿ᵉnšūf‿ᵉšwayy.	– Not those. The book that's next to the exercise books. It's white <its color [is] white>, isn't it? Bring it and draw back the curtain from the window <move the curtain from ...> so that we can see a bit.
– la', fīʰ šams‿ᵉktīr il-yōm biddī-š azīḥ il-burdāy.	– No, it's very sunny <there's a lot of sun> today, I don't want to open <move> the curtain.
– ᵉmbala, zīḥ-ha[5] šwayy!	– Come on <yes you do>, open it <move it> a bit.

– biddi aqul-lak 'iši.	– I want to tell you something.
– tfaḍḍal.	– Go ahead! <please [do]>.
– la-mīn il-busuklēt illi barra jamb il-bāb?	– Whose bicycle is that <to-whom [is] the bicycle that > [is] outside beside the door?
– hāda la-'aḫūy.	– It's my brother's <that [is] to-my-brother>

---

5. zīḥ-ha is usually pronounced zīḥḥa (the h is assimilated into the ḥ).

– q**u**l-lo: miš l**ā**zem ik**ū**n h**ē**k b**ɑ**rrɑ fi-š-š**a**ms.	– Tell him it shouldn't be outside <it must not be> in the sun like that.
– ṭ**ɑ**yyeb, baq**u**l-lo. š**ū** kam**ā**n? f**ī**^{h} '**i**ši t**ā**ni?	– OK, I'll tell him. What next <what also>? Is there anything else <another thing>?
– '**a**ywa, q**u**l-li w**ē**n muft**ā**ḥ il-b**ē**t, muš m**a**^{c}ak?	– Yes. Tell me where the house key is. Haven't you got it <[is it] not with you>?
– l**a**', muš m**a**^{c}i.	– No, I haven't got it.
– ma^c m**ī**n bik**ū**n hal-muft**ā**ḥ?	– Who's got that key <with whom will be...>?
– 'ab**ū**y biq**ū**l inno‿l-muft**ā**ḥ ^{c}ind il-jir**ɑ̄**n fi-l-m**ɑ**ṭbɑḫ.	– My father says that the key's at the neighbors' [house], in the kitchen.
– ṭ**ɑ**yyeb, r**ū**ḥ j**ī**bo qaw**ɑ̄**m. u-ba^{c}d**ē**n f**ū**t la-j**u**wwa.	– Fine, go and get it straight away, then <and afterwards> come indoors!

– haz-z**a**lame ^{c}**i**ndo ul**ā**d‿^{e}kt**ī**r: '**a**rba^c ul**ā**d u-ḫ**a**m^{e}s ban**ā**t.[6]	– This man has a lot of <many> children: four boys and five girls.
– h**ā**da Mun**ī**r, w**ā**ḥad min ewl**ā**do.	– This is Munir, one of his children.
hal-w**a**lad ^{c}**i**ndo '**i**ḫwe u-ḫaw**ā**t:	This boy has brothers and sisters.
h**ā**da mn**ī**ḥ; ^{c}**i**ndo	That's good! He's got
t**a**lat '**i**ḫwe u-ḫ**a**m^{e}s ḫaw**ā**t.	three brothers and five sisters.
bir**ū**ḥ ^{c}a-l-m**a**drase ma^c ḫaw**ā**to	He goes to school with his sisters
k**u**ll y**ō**m eṣ-ṣ**u**b^{o}ḥ,	every day in the morning.
u-ab**ū**-hom bir**ū**ḥ ^{c}a-š-š**u**ġ^{o}l	And their father goes to work with his
ma^c ewl**ā**do l-^{e}kb**ɑ̄**r.[7]	older <big> children.
– l-^{e}kb**ɑ̄**r ma birūḥ**ū**-š ^{c}a-l-m**a**drase?	– Don't the older children go to school <the big [ones] don't go to the school> ?
– l**a**', birūḥu m**a**^{c}o ^{c}a-š-š**u**ġ^{o}l.	– No, they go with him to work.
– b**i**ddi ar**ū**ḥ az**ū**r-hom,	– I want to go and visit them.
ma bidd**a**k-š‿^{e}tš**ū**f-hom	Don't you want to see them too
'**i**nte (-ta) kam**ā**n?	<you don't want to see them you also>?
– ^{e}mb**a**la, bar**ū**ḥ m**a**^{c}ek.	– Of course I do. I'll go with you.
– '**i**za h**ē**k, '**a**na kam**ā**n bar**ū**ḥ m**a**^{c}kom.	– If that's the case <if thus>, I'll go with you, too.
– tf**ɑ**ḍḍɑl.	– Please do!

---

6. We'll discuss what happens when a number is followed by a noun, very soon.

7. This is the plural form of kb**ī**r.

Explanations

1. I have / I've got (here with me; at home)

Take care to distinguish between:

ᶜindak muftāḥ?	*Have you got a key* (somewhere or other)?
maᶜak muftāḥ?	*Have you got a key* (on you at the moment: in your pocket, in your hand)?
il-muftāḥ maᶜak?	*Have you got the key* (with you / in your pocket, etc.)?

2. You will see; she will see

As we have already pointed out (in **Lesson 5, Explanations 3**), the Arabic form beṭšūf indicates both the 2nd person masculine singular (*you* m sing *see / will see*) and the 3rd person feminine singular (*she sees / will see*).

lāzem‿etzūr 'immak	*You must visit your mother*
or	*She must visit your mother*

The sentence above is, therefore, ambiguous, and it is only the context that tells us whether to understand it as meaning *you must......* or *she must......* If we need to make things unambiguously clear, we can add the personal pronoun before or after the verb:

'iza beṭšūfo 'inte	*If you see him...*
'iza hiyye beṭšūfo	*If she sees him...*

3. illi – that, who / inno – that

According to the **Vocabulary** list on page 40, the English word *that* translates into Arabic as both inno and illi, according to meaning and context:

When *that* means *which* (*the thing that...*), we use the Arabic word illi;

Note that illi also means *who* in sentences like *the man who brings milk every day* (see below).

When *that* is used as a conjunction (in expressions like *he said that...* or *he knows that...*) the Arabic word inno is used.

A few examples will help to illustrate this:

iz-zalame **illi** bijīb ḥalīb kull yōm	*The man **who** brings milk every day*
biqūl **inno** ma fi-šš ḥalīb il-yōm.	*says **that** there is no milk today.*
biqūl inno‿l-muftāḥ miš hōn	*He says that the key isn't here*
biddo‿l-muftāḥ illi fi-l-ḫazāne	*He wants the key that's in the cupboard.*

Exercises

A. Translate into English:

1. la-mīn hal-ᵉktāb?
2. il-muftāḥ muš maᶜo.
3. šūf! il-muftāḥ ᶜala‿l-bāb.
4. il-kursi jamb iš-šubbāk.
5. wēn ħawātak? – humme fi-l-mαṭbαħ.
6. biddi ašūf ’uħtak l-ᵉkbīre qabl‿is-sēᶜa ᶜašαrα.
7. ᶜindi šuġᵒl minšān-ha.
8. ṭαyyeb, baqul-lha (pronounce: baqulha).
9. ma fīʰ šams il-yōm.
10. šū lōn il-bᾱṣ? – ’ayya bᾱṣ? fīʰ bᾱṣ ’aḥmαr u-fīʰ bᾱṣ ’azrαq.
11. zīḥ (move!) ᶜan iš-šubbāk, biddi ašūf iš-šams.

B. Complete the sentences

(Replace the English words with the appropriate expression in Arabic):

12. šū (the color of) il-bāb?
13. šū lōn (the door of the house)?
14. jib-li jarīdc (before) trūḥ.
15. (When) biddak‿ᵉtrūḥ (to school)?
16. He can’t (not possible) irūḥ hallaq (there’s no bus).

C. Translate into Arabic:

17. There’s a man here, he wants to see you^{f}.
18. What does he want from me (minni), this man?
19. He says that you’ve got the school key (on you / in your pocket).
20. That’s not true, the key’s on the table in the kitchen.
21. The table that’s in the kitchen……
22. The chair’s outside in the sun.
23. The chairs at the school <that [are] in the school>.
24. Bring the newspapers that are on the table!
25. See if the bicycle is indoors or outdoors (or = willa).
26. That’s enough. This lesson has tired me out <I’m tired from this lesson>.

What about the "sun letters"? (An additional exercise)

When does the -l of the definite article il- change into the first letter of the word that follows it? Take another look at **Lesson 2**, **Explanations 1**, then do the following exercise: put the definite article il- in front of the following words that we have learned in lessons 1-7.

27.	k**u**rsi	mαṣ**ᾱ**ri	ṭ**ᾱ**wle	fikrα
28.	mαr**ī**ḍ	d**a**ftαr	m**a**drase	n**ā**s
29.	z**a**lame	m**α**ṭbαḫ	s**ē**^{c}a	d**ᾱ**r

id-dars it-tāmen

8

The Eighth Lesson

Now we're going to leave verbs of the **šūf** / **jīb** type behind for a while and take a look at the verb **ka**tab (*he wrote*) in order to learn the **past tense.**

Y**ū**sef k**a**tab makt**ū**b	*Yusef wrote a letter*
š**ū** kat**a**b-t, ya Y**ū**sef?	*What did you write, Yusef?*
kat**a**b-t il-makt**ū**b	*I wrote the letter.*
š**ū** kat**a**b-ti, ya M**a**ryam?	*What did you write, Maryam?*
kat**a**b-t id-d**a**rs.	*I wrote the lesson*

Two comments:

The 1st person of the verb (*I),* has the same form as its 2nd person **masculine**, (*you*m), and both are created by adding a -t to the 3rd person masculine singular form of the past tense: ('**a**na) kat**a**b-t = ('**i**nte) kat**a**b-t ….

- Note that when this -t is added, the stress moves from the **first** syllable of the word to the **second**:

k**a**-tab + -t → ka-t**a**b-t

Here is the complete paradigm of the verb in the past tense:

kat**a**b-t or kat**a**bet[1]	*I wrote*	k**a**tab	*he wrote*
kat**a**b-t or kat**a**bet[1]	*you*m *wrote*		
kat**a**b-ti	*you*f *wrote*	k**a**tb-at	*she wrote*
kat**a**b-na	*we wrote*		
kat**a**b-tu	*you*m/f pl	k**a**tabu	*they wrote*

Note that in the paradigm above all the 3rd person forms (*he*, *she* and *they*) are arranged in a separate column, as, in the past tense, they all have **something in common** that sets them apart from the 1st and 2nd persons; this "something" is the position of the stressed syllable:

In all the 3rd person forms (*he, she, they*) the stress falls on the **first** syllable
In all the other forms in this paradigm, the stress falls on the syllable **just before the suffix** (-t, -ti, -na, -tu).

---

1. In accordance with the same rule that applies to bint / binet. See **Explanations 2** on page 15.

> In **the past tense of all the verbs** the 3rd person will always differ in some way from the 1st and the 2 nd persons

Vocabulary

b-	with, by means of	ṭɑlɑb	he asked for / requested
maᶜ	with, together with[2]	'aħad	he took / received / got
ṭōše	fight, brawl	ḍɑrɑb	he hit / struck / beat
maraq	he passed by	maħzan [maħāzen]	storeroom
tarak	he left / abandoned	jumᶜa [jumaᶜ]	week
qatal	he killed	'usbūᶜ ['asābīᶜ]	week
sa'al	he asked (a question)	jōz	husband

miskīn (maskīn) [masākīn] poor (in both senses: both *unfortunate* and *hard up*)
sakat he kept quiet / fell silent / said nothing / shut up
mawjūd present, in (as in *he's in at the moment*).

Conversation

– 'immi 'issa mawjūde fi 'Amērka, katbat maktūb min hunāk qabᵉl jumᶜa, u-aħad-na‿l-maktūb il-yōm iṣ-ṣuboḥ.[3]	– My mother's in America at the moment <my mother now [is] present in America> She wrote a letter from there a week ago <before a week>, and we got the letter this morning <today the morning>.
– 'ana kamān katabᵉt maktūb.	– I've written a letter, too
– kīf katabt‿il-maktūb? ᶜal-mākina willa bil-qalam?	– How did you write the letter <how you wrote the letter>? On the typewriter <on the machine> or with a pen?

2. Unlike English, Arabic distinguishes between b- (*with* in the sense of *by means of*) and maᶜ (*with* in the sense of *together with*). In Arabic no one cuts *with* a knife, only *by means of* a knife.

3. ṣuboḥ / ṣubeḥ is the usual word for *morning*. The word ṣɑbāḥ is used in greetings such as ṣɑbāḥ in-nūr

– b-il-q**a**lam, ma ^{c}ind**ī**-š m**ā**kina (m**ā**kana).	– With a pen. I haven't got a typewriter.

– š**ū** haṣ-ṣy**ɑ̄**ḥ, š**ū** haṭ-ṭ**ō**še, š**ū** fī^{h} b**ɑ**rrɑ?	– What's all that shouting? What's the fuss about <that brawl>, what's happening outside <what is there outside>?
– il-ewl**ā**d ḍ**ɑ**rɑbu… ya^{c}ni…	– The children hit… I mean <it means>…
– ḍ**ɑ**rɑbu m**ī**n? r**ū**ḥ š**ū**f, u-ba^{c}d**ē**n q**u**l-li.	– Whom did they hit <they hit whom>? Go and see <go see>, then <afterwards> tell me.

(He comes back:)

– Y**ū**sef ḍ**ɑ**rɑb 'u**ḫ**to M**a**ryam?	– Did Yusef hit his sister Maryam?
– l**a**', h**ī** ḍ**ɑ**rbat 'aḫ**ū**-ha;[4] '**a**na sa'**a**lt il-b**i**nt…	– No, she hit her brother; I asked the girl…
– h**ɑ̄**, sa'**a**lt-ha?	– Ah, did you ask her?
– '**a**ywa, sa'**a**lt: l**ē**š ḍ**ɑ**r**ɑ**bti Y**ū**sef, bass h**i**yye s**a**ktat.	– Yes, I asked, "Why did you hit Yusef," but she said nothing.
– h**ɑ̄**, h**ā**da dal**ī**l inno h**i**yye illi (h**i**yye‿lli) ḍ**ɑ**rbato.	– Aha, that's proof < a sign> that it was her who hit him <that she [was] who hit him>.
– mɑẓb**ū**ṭ!	– Exactly!

'iḥna
sāknīn fi
nafs iš-šāre^{c}

---

4. We are already familiar with the forms **'aḫu-** (*brother-of*) and **'aḫūy** (*my brother*).

– fīʰ hōn zalame.	– There’s a man here.
– mīn huwwe? šū biddo?	– Who [is] he? What does he want?
– hāda‿z-zalame illi ṭɑlɑb il-muftāḥ ᵉmbēreḥ.	– This is the man who asked for the key yesterday.
– ’ayya muftāḥ?	– Which key?
– muftāḥ il-maḫzan.	– The key to the storeroom <key-of the st.>.
– hɑ̄, šu biddo‿l-yōm?	– Ah! What does he want today?
– maraq fi-š-šāreᶜ u-immi kamān marqat fi nafs[5] iš-šāreᶜ u-huwwe sa’al kīf ḥālak u-wēnak. sa’al ’iza ’inte fi-l-bēt.	– He was passing by in the street, and my mother was going along <passing by in> the same street, and he asked how you were[6] and where you were. He asked if you were at home.
– sa’alto šu biddo?	– Did you ask him what he wanted <wants>?
– ’ɑ̄, sa’alto.	– Yes, I did <yes I asked him>.
– ṭɑlɑb minnak ’iši?	– Did he ask you for anything <from you a thing>?
– la’, wala ’iši.	– No, nothing <no thing>.

– id-doktōr biqūl inno jɑ̄ro qatal ḥālo.[5]	– The doctor says that his neighbor has killed himself.
– lēš?	– Why?
– ᶜašān mɑrɑto[7] tarkato.	– Because his wife has left him.
– bass huwwe‿lli tarak mɑrɑto u-tarak ’ewlādo.	– But he’s [the one] who left his wife and <left his> children.

---

5. See below, **Explanations 2.**

6. Note that while in English we have to say *He asked how you **were**,* in Arabic you must say *He asked how you are* <he asked how [is] your condition>.

7. jōz = husband and mɑrɑ = woman; wife. *My wife* in Arabic is mɑrɑti. What’s the -t- doing here? You’ll get a full answer in Lesson 21.

– **la**’, **hi**yye‿lli **ta**rkat	– No, she’s the one who abandoned
’ewl**ā**d-ha u-j**ō**z-ha.	her children and her husband.
u-sa’**a**lt-ha: l**ē**š tar**a**kti	And I asked her, “Why did you leave
j**ō**zek w-ewl**ā**dek?	your husband and your children?”
saktat.	She said nothing.
– mask**ī**n (misk**ī**n) haz-**za**lame!	– Poor man <poor, that man>!
’**α**llα **yir**ḥamo!	God rest his soul <[may] God pity him>!

Explanations

1. Stress

Have you noticed that, in all the verbs taught in this lesson, the stress moves from the first syllable to the second?

sa’al → sa’**a**l-t   **ḍα**rαb → ḍαr**α**bti   **ta**rak → tar**a**kti

Listen to the recording again, and pay special attention to these changes. That’ll do for today. We’ll explain things at length in Lesson 14.

2. “Myself”; “the same”

Now let’s go back and take another look at some of the things we’ve discovered today:

1. The word ḥ**ā**l, which means *condition / situation* (k**ī**f ḥ**ā**lak?), is also used to form the expressions *myself, yourself*, etc. **qa**tal ḥ**ā**lo = *he killed himself.* It likewise appears in the expression la-ḥ**ā**li, which means *by myself / on my own.* Here are some examples:

I wrote it myself / by myself / on my own	kat**a**bto la-ḥ**ā**li
Did you$^{\text{m sing}}$ *write the letter yourself?*	kat**a**bt il-makt**ū**b la-ḥ**ā**lak?
I go in by myself.	baf**ū**t la-ḥ**ā**li
Go$^{\text{f sing}}$ *on your own!*	r**ū**ḥi la-ḥ**ā**lek

Take care to pronounce the ḥ- sound properly (i.e., not like the *ch* in the word *loch*). If you don’t get it right, people will think you’re talking about your maternal uncle (ђ**ā**l)!

2. The word **na**fs, which means *soul*, can likewise be used to form the expressions *myself, yourself*; b-**na**fso means *by himself* . When placed **before** a noun, however, **na**fs means *[the] same*:

in the same house	fi **na**fs il-b**ē**t
the same key	**na**fs il-muft**āḥ**
in the same color	b-**na**fs il-l**ō**n
the same thing	**na**fs iš-š**ī**[8]

Exercises

A. Translate into English:

1. h**ā**da **na**fs il-muft**āḥ**
2. h**ā**da‿z-z**a**lame illi k**a**tab il-makt**ū**b.
3. w**ē**n il-w**a**lad illi ḍ**ɑ**rɑbak?
4. bif**ū**t ᶜala b**ē**t il-jir**ɑ̄**n.
5. hal-m**ɑ**rɑ bitr**ūḥ** ᶜala‿s-s**ī**nama maᶜ j**ō**z-ha.
6. misk**ī**ne, ’**i**mmi s**ā**kne hun**ā**k la-ḥ**ā**l-ha.
7. l**ā**zem‿ᵉtz**ū**r-ha kull y**ō**m.
8. ’aђ**ū**y muš mawj**ū**d, t**a**rak il-b**ē**t il-y**ō**m iṣ-ṣ**u**bᵒḥ.

B. Complete the sentences

(Replace the English words with the appropriate expression in Arabic):

9. ’**i**ḥna s**ā**kn**ī**n (in the same house).
10. il-y**ō**m kam**ā**n k**a**tab (the same letter).
11. ’**i**nti kat**a**bti‿l-makt**ū**b (yourself f sing)?
12. ’**i**nte kat**a**bt il-makt**ū**b (yourself m sing)?
13. ’**a**ywa, ’**a**na kat**a**bto (myself).
14. ’**a**na ṭɑl**ɑ**bᵉt d**a**ftɑr ’**a**zrɑq u-h**u**wwe ṭ**ɑ**lɑb (the same thing).
15. y**a**ᶜni, (the same exercise book in the same color).
16. ’**i**mmi (asked for) mɑṣ**ɑ̄**ri min ’ab**ū**y.
17. b**i**ddo ir**ūḥ** ᶜala ḥ**ē**fa u-iz**ū**r ᶜ**a**kka[9] (on the same day).

C. Translate into Arabic:

18. He asked my mother, and my mother asked[10] my father.

---

8. The Arabic for *thing* is **šī** (š**a**y’ in literary Arabic) or ’**i**ši. With the definite article we say iš-š**ī** or il-’**i**ši. h**ā**da **na**fs iš-š**ī** = *That’s the same thing.*

9. The town of Acre (Acco).

10. *She asked* = **sa**’alat or **sa**’lat (’ represents a glottal stop – i.e., a sudden pause in speech).

19. She asked him, but he said nothing.
20. He asked my sister if there was milk in the kitchen <if there is milk…..>.
21. I asked the boy: "How old are you <how much is your age>?"
22. Our neighbor hit his son.
23. We asked our neighbor why he had hit <why he hit> his son.
24. Yesterday you^{pl} passed by our house.
25. [That's] right <true>, we passed by in the street and asked where you lived <where you live>.
26. What color is the door of the house <[the] color [of the] door-of the house>?

You can do this exercise in writing, but it's a good idea to compare the result with the **Key to the Exercises** on page 117, then read the correct translation out loud.

Just to satisfy your curiosity

You are probably already asking yourselves why some verbs are written with an a, while others are written with an ɑ (s**a**kat – ṭ**ɑ**lɑb). The answer is simple: because of the type of consonants they contain (and this applies to **all words**, not just verbs). "Emphatic" or "dark" consonants such as ṣ, ḍ, ṭ and z, and sometimes r, too, affect the sound of the nearby vowels and "require" a "dark" back ɑ sound (see **Vowels**, p. [12]). In other words, s**a**kat and ṭ**ɑ**lɑb are not two different types of verb: it is merely the presence of the ṭ- that turns the two a-s into ɑ-s. If you go back and look over all the words we've learned so far, you'll see that this is a generalized phenomenon. See, for example:

w**a**lad	as opposed to	m**ɑ**rɑ	bik**a**ffi	as opposed to	ṭ**ɑ**yyeb
b**ā**b	as opposed to	d**ɑ̄**r	s**ā**ken	as opposed to	š**ɑ̄**ṭer
j**u**wwa	as opposed to	b**ɑ**rrɑ			

And, of course, there are also exceptions that have to be remembered individually: qaw**ɑ̄**m[11] (*quickly / straight away*), b**ɑ̄**bɑ (*daddy / papa*), m**ɑ̄**mɑ (*mummy / mommy / mama*) and, most important of all, 'ɑll**ɑ̄**h or '**ɑ**llɑ (*God*).

---

11. You may also hear qaw**ā**m.

id-dars it-tāse^c

9

The Ninth Lesson

Here are a few more sentences and exercises using the same verbs, before we move on to new material.

Vocabulary

ḥada[1] / ḥadd	anyone, anybody	ḥarb	war
ma-ḥada	nobody, no one	salām	peace
ma-ḥadā-š / ma-ḥadd-š	nobody	^caql / ^caq^el	mind, sense, intelligence
mawḍū^c	subject, topic	maṣ^er	Egypt
daqīqa [daqāyeq]	minute	maṣri	Egyptian
daḫal	he went in / entered	yimken	perhaps
il-^cālam	the world	ša^cb / ša^c^eb	(a) people
dafa^c	he paid / made [someone] do [something] / pushed [someone]		
qahwe	coffee; café, coffee house		

Conversation

Fi-l-qahwe — In the café

This conversation would appear to have taken place before 1973. Mr. Haddad – Yusef and Maryam's father – and Dr. Elias are sitting in a coffee house. The waiter, who has forgotten what they ordered, comes back to inquire:

– šū ṭalabtu?	– What did you order?
– 'ana ṭalab^et bīra	– I ordered a beer,
w-il-'ustāz[2] ṭalab qahwe,	and this gentleman ordered coffee,
u-ṭalabna kamān ka^c^ek.[3]	and we also ordered cakes.
– hallaq bajīb il-kull,	– I'll bring everything right away.
bass daqīqa / bass‿^edqīqa.	Just a minute.

---

1. This word is usually used in a question: *Has anyone come? / Did you see anyone?* or in a conditional sentence *(If anyone asks you...).*

2. 'ustāz is an honorific title used to address a teacher, a university lecturer, a doctor or any other highly-educated male.

3. Also bagels and other baked goods.

– yā 'ustāz Elyās,	– Dr Elias <oh professor Elias>,
šū biqūlu fi-r-rɑ̄dyo?	what are they saying on the radio?
– ya sīdi, mɑṣᵉr bid-ha hɑrb.	– Sir, Egypt wants war.
– **la'**, **la'**, miš mumken!	– No, no, [that's] impossible!
– ᵉmbala, rūsya	– It's perfectly possible <yes it is>. Russia
dafᶜat mɑṣᵉr la-l-ḥɑrb.	has pushed Egypt towards war.
– ya zalame, wēn ᶜaqlak[4]?	– [Come on], man, where's your [common] sense?
muš maᶜqul[4] hāda!	It doesn't make sense <not logical, that [thing]>!
rūsya (ma) bidhā-š ḥɑrb.	Russia doesn't want war.
– 'ana muš maᶜak	– I don't agree with you <I'm not with you>
fi hal-mawḍūᶜ.	on this topic.
– iš-šaᶜb il-mɑṣri mā-biddo ḥɑrb.	– The Egyptian people don't <doesn't> want war.
il-yōm ma-ḥadā-š / ma-ḥadd-š biddo ḥɑrb fi-l-ᶜālam.	Today nobody in the world wants war.
kull wāḥad biddo salām!	Everyone wants peace!
– yaᶜni… yimken maᶜak ḥaqq.	– Well, perhaps you're right <it is possible [that] there is with you rightness>.
ᶜala kull ḥāl, lāzem‿ᵉnrūḥ.	In any case, we've got to go.
yɑllɑ,[5] b-ḫɑ̄ṭer-kom.[6]	Let's go! See you later.

---

4. It's not difficult to pronounce ᶜaqlak: first you say ᶜa-, then you pause, then you say lak with a descending intonation. The word maᶜqul is from the same root (ᶜ-q-l). For more about the **Arabic root**, see p.61.

5. yā 'ɑllɑ̄h = Oh God! This is an appeal for help in times of effort, and the shortened form yɑllɑ, by extension, means *Come on! / Let's get going! / Heave-ho!* Listen carefully to the recording and you will notice that the ll- is pronounced in an "emphatic" manner and is "dark" like the Russian *l-* of *balalaika* or the *-ll* of the English word *all*. As a result the *a* sounds are also "dark."

6. See **Explanations 1**, below.

The waiter:

– dafa^ctu ḥaqq[7] il-bīra w-il-qahwe? ma-ḥadā-š dafa^c!	– Have you paid for <have you paid the price-of> the beer and the coffee? No one's paid!
– ^embala, 'ana dafa^cet!	– Yes [we have], **I've** paid!
– 'ah, maẓbūṭ.	– Ah, right….

They leave

– ᵉmnīḥ illi[8] tarakna mawḍūᶜ il-ḥarb.	– It's a good thing we dropped the subject of war <good that we left…>
– 'aywa. ṭayyeb, b-ḫāṭrak[9] ya 'abu Yūsef.[10]	– Yes. Well, see you soon Abu Yusef.
– maᶜ is-salāme.[9]	– Goodbye.

---

7. Apart from *justice, truth, right,* ḥaqq also means *price* (i.e., the *right* to the beer once you've paid for it), and so hāda, šu ḥaqqo? means *How much is it* <that, what is its price>?

8. In expressions of satisfaction, happiness, contentment and other emotions (*It's good that / I'm happy that / It's a pity that,* etc.) the word *that* is expressed by illi (not inno): *I'm glad that it's you who paid!* translates into Arabic as **'ana mabsūṭ illi dafaᶜtu 'intu!** <I'm glad that you paid, you!>.

9. See below, **Explanations 1.**

10. See below **Explanations 2**.

– ᵉmbēreḥ maraṭi daħlat	– Yesterday my wife went
ᶜa-s-supermarket	into the supermarket
u-s**a**'lat qadd**ēš** ḥ**a**qq il-ḥal**ī**b.	and asked how much the milk cost <how much [is] the price of the milk>.
u-baᶜdēn d**a**fᶜat u-**a**ħdat il-ḥal**ī**b	Then <and afterwards> she paid and took
la-ᶜind '**i**mmi.	the milk to my mother's.
– lēš, il-ḥal**ī**b muš ᶜaš**ā**n-ku?	– Why? Wasn't the milk for you <the milk [is] not for you>?
– l**a**', '**i**mmi ṭalbat min maraṭi	– No. My mother [had] asked my wife
inn-ha‿tjīb ḥal**ī**b u-ħ**u**bᵉz.	to bring milk and bread.

Explanations

1. See you soon / Au revoir!

b-ħ**ā**ṭr-ak means *with your permission* – in other words: *permit me to take my leave of you.* This is what you say when you leave a place and say goodbye to your friend and / or host. When addressing a woman or girl you say b-ħ**ā**ṭrek. The proper response to this leave-taking formula is maᶜ is-sal**ā**me, which means *[go] in peace* <with peace / safety / health>.

The word ħ**ā**ṭer means *desire / inclination.* When the possessive pronoun -ak or -ek is attached to it, the vowel -e- is dropped. Before the attached pronoun -ku / -kom, however, the -e- is retained, and this actually becomes the stressed syllable (we'll see why later on). When we take our leave of more than one person, we say b-ħāṭ**er**-kom!

When you leave, you say:

... and your friend replies:

But if he/she speaks first and says

you reply:

'**ɑ**llɑ is**a**llmak, or →
<God preserve you>

which will be explained later

2. Abu Yusef

It is customary to address a father by the name of his eldest son – '**a**bu Y**ū**sef <father-of Yusef>, '**a**bu '**A**ḥmad etc., even if this son is not the firstborn child, i.e., if he has an elder sister or sisters – and even if he has not yet been born! When a son is born, he'll be given the name that has been "waiting" for him. In the same way, the mother is referred to as '**i**mm Y**ū**sef.

3. Numbers

It's time to talk about the numbers in Arabic.

Here is the list of the cardinal numbers (*one, two, three*) and ordinal numbers (*first, second, third*) from 1 to 10.

■ 1	w**ā**ḥed/w**ā**ḥad	*first*	'**a**wwal
2	tn**ē**n/t^{e}n**ē**n	*second*	t**ā**ni
3	tal**ā**te / tl**ā**te	*third*	t**ā**let
4	'**a**rb^{c}a / '**a**rba^{c}a	*fourth*	r**ɑ̄**be^{c}
5	ђ**a**mse	*fifth*	ђ**ā**mes
6	s**i**tte	*sixth*	s**ā**des
7	s**a**b^{c}a	*seventh*	s**ā**be^{c}
8	tam**ā**nye / tm**ā**nye	*eighth*	t**ā**men
9	t**i**s^{c}a	*ninth*	t**ā**se^{c}
10	^{c}**a**šɑrɑ	*tenth*	^{c}**ā**šer

Don't forget to read out the page number each time you start a new page. From page 35 onwards we have indicated only the "tens" (*thirty, forty, fifty*, etc.), as you can work out for yourself how to say 43, 57, 79, etc. We have already explained on page 23 that in Arabic we say *one and twenty*, and so, similarly, we say *three and forty, seven and fifty* and *nine and seventy*. In the future you will be able to do a new exercise: you can open the book at random, look at the page number, and say the Arabic number out loud.

We have already come across expressions such as '**ar**ba^{c} ul**ā**d, ħ**a**m^{e}s ban**ā**t, in which the numbers take a different form from those in the table above. What is the rule?

– Numbers between 3 and 10 lose their final syllable when they come before the noun that is being counted; the noun itself is in the plural.

Read out loud:

■3	tal**ā**te	**ta**lat kαr**ā**si	*three chairs*
4	'**ar**b(a)^{c}a	'**ar**ba^{c} maf**ā**t**ī**ḥ	*four keys*
5	ħ**a**mse	ħ**a**m^{e}s daq**ā**yeq	*five minutes*
6	s**i**tte	s**i**tt k**u**tob	*six books*
7	s**a**b^{c}a	s**a**b^{e}^{c} ban**ā**t	*seven girls*
8	tam**ā**nye	t**a**man 'iħwe	*eight brothers*
9	t**i**s^{c}a	t**i**s^{e}^{c} / t**i**s^{a}^{c} ul**ā**d	*nine children*
10	^{c}**a**šαrα	^{c}**a**š^{e}r ħaw**ā**t	*ten sisters*

'**i**za w**ā**ḥad ^{c}**i**ndo t**i**s^{e}^{c} ul**ā**d, kull w**a**lad ^{c}**i**ndo t**a**man '**i**ħwe.
If someone has nine sons, each child has eight brothers.

You will have noticed that each of these numbers is "shortened." For example, **ta**lat (or tlat / talt) and **ta**man have lost their long syllable, while the numbers 5, 7, 9 and 10, which are "officially" ħ**a**ms, s**a**b^{c}, t**i**s^{c} and ^{c}**a**šr, have acquired an extra ^{e} like that of b**i**nt →b**i**n^{e}t. But now let's see how this works in "real life." Read the third column out loud once more – u-bik**a**ffi!

We've dealt with the numbers 3-10. What about 1 and 2?

–The number *one* is used **after** the noun when you want emphasize that a single person / object is under discussion: w**a**lad w**ā**ḥad = *one boy* (and no more than one). This number has a feminine form, too: *one girl* = b**i**nt w**ā**ḥde / w**a**ḥade.

– The number *two*, when it stands alone (i.e., without an accompanying noun) also has a masculine form (tnēn, tᵉnēn) and a feminine form (tintēn).

– But what happens when the number 2 is accompanied by a noun: *2 boys, 2 girls, 2 books*, etc? In this case we use the **dual** form in Arabic, which is formed by adding -ēn to the noun:

2 boys	waladēn	*2 girls*	bintēn
2 books	ktābēn	*2 buses*	bɑ̄ṣēn

One final important comment:

Please note: any noun that follows a number between 11 and 99 will always **be in the singular.** This is not as strange as it sounds: in certain dialects of English, too, we still hear expressions such as *nigh on forty year.* In Arabic we say 'arbaᶜ dafāter (*four exercise books*) but 'arbaᶜ u-ᶜišrīn daftɑr (*twenty-four exercise books*).

So how do you say *thirty children*? That's right, talātīn walad. As for what happens from 100 onwards, we'll learn about that when we reach page 107.

4. The feminine ending

Here is the explanation we promised in one of the previous lessons, just to satisfy your curiosity:

Although most words in the feminine end in -e, some end in -a / -ɑ. When does this happen? When the final consonant before the suffix is "dark" or emphatic (the emphatic consonants are ḍ, ṭ, ṣ, ẓ), or if it is a consonant produced far back in the throat: ᶜ, ġ, ḥ, ħ and, in some circumstances, r, too. To illustrate this, let's take a look at the numbers from 3 to 10:

talāte 'arbᶜa* ħamse sitte sabᶜa* tamānye tisᶜa* ᶜašɑrɑ**

* back of the throat ** -r-

Now you can go back and look at all the words we've learned since the first lesson, and you'll understand, for example, why we say taᶜbāne and mabsūṭɑ.[11]

---

11. In the villages around Jerusalem and the Gaza Strip there is a tendency to pronounce the ending -e as -a. Some people there say madrasa, while others say madrase. Nonetheless, you would do well to learn to pronounce these words as recommended in this book.

Reminder! You don't need to remember these linguistic explanations. While it's important that you **understand** the explanations, you don't have to learn them off by heart. With time you'll learn the rules simply by constantly applying them.

Exercises

A. Translate into English:

1. ᶜ**i**ndi walad**ē**n: w**a**lad u-b**i**nᵉt.
2. il-w**a**lad, qadd**ē**š ᶜ**u**mro? – s**a**ne u-n**u**ṣṣ.
3. w-il-b**i**nt, qadd**ē**š ᶜ**u**mᵉr-ha?
4. ḫ**a**ms‿ᵉsn**ī**n.
5. m**a**raq min h**ō**n q**a**bᵉl s**ē**ᶜa.
6. ’**i**mmi miš mawj**ū**de; b**i**ddak‿ᵉtš**ū**f ’ab**ū**y?
7. f**ī**ʰ ḥ**a**da b**ɑ**rrɑ?
8. ’**i**ḥna s**ā**kn**ī**n fi n**a**fs‿il-b**ē**t.
9. t**a**rak il-busukl**ē**t (baskal**ē**t) j**a**mb il-m**a**ḫzan.

B. Complete the sentences

(Replace the English words with the appropriate expression in Arabic):

10. [Did] ḥ**a**da (ask) m**i**nnak il-muft**ā**ḥ?
11. l**a**’, (no one) ṭ**ɑ**lɑb m**i**nni ’**i**ši.
12. [Did] j**ɑ̄**rna (ask you) w**ē**n ’ab**ū**k? – l**a**’, (he asked) ’**i**mmi.
13. (we asked) il-muḫt**ɑ̄**r (if there [was] <is> a) b**ɑ̄**ṣ. q**ā**l: m**ā**-fīʰ.
14. ’**ē**š (did you^{pl} ask) m**i**nni (yesterday)?
15. biq**ū**l (that you are)[12] ’**i**bn‿il-muḫt**ɑ̄**r.
16. h**ā**da l-ᵉkt**ā**b, (how much does it cost <[is] its price>)?

C. Translate into Arabic:

17. The bus has just gone by <now went by the bus>.
18. No one has been by <has passed by from> here.
19. Who wrote this letter?

---

12. The English conjunction *that* = inno, or inn- with the addition of the attached pronouns -i , -ak, etc., depending on the subject of the sentence:
He says that you're hard-working / bright = biq**ū**l inno ’**i**nte š**ɑ̄**ṭer / biq**ū**l inn-ak š**ɑ̄**ṭer. *It's best that she go on her own* = ’**a**ḥsan inn-ha tr**ū**ḥ la-ḥ**ā**l-ha.

20. No one wrote to my father.
21. I asked him for money <I asked from him money>. He asked her for money.
22. Do you want coffee?
23. I don't want coffee now <now I don't want....>,
    I've got to go <it's necessary that I go>.
24. That man's got a lot of sense <this man, his mind is big>.
25. He always says, "We don't want shouting <shouts> or <and> a fight."
26. We want peace here and all over the world <in all the world>.

If you can't say all this, don't worry! Compare your attempts with the **Key to the Exercises** on page 118.

The Arabic Root

You will almost certainly have noticed that the words katab, maktūb and ktāb all have something in common: the letters k-t-b, which constitute the **root** shared by all three of them. In Arabic, roots consist of three (or, less often, four) *consonants* that serve as a form of "scaffolding" for the vowels inserted among them to create the various word patterns. Vowels do not usually form part of the root. For example, the plural of ktāb is [kutob] – the vowels change, but the root remains the same.

We'll make do with this simple explanation for the time being - more later!

id-dars il-ᶜāšer

10

The Tenth Lesson

Let's hope you haven't forgotten our old friends šūf, jīb, rūḥ, kūn and zūr, as the time has come to take a look at what happens to them in the **past** tense. As with the conjugation of **all verbs** in Arabic, here, too, we add the now-familiar endings:

1st / 2nd person	– –t	– –t	– –ti	– –na	– –tu
3rd person		– –	– –at		– –u

These are exactly the same endings that we used with the verb k**a**tab. But let's see, first of all, what happens in the 3rd person:

■ Present Yūsef bizūr il-jirān k**u**ll yōm — *Yusef visits the neigbors every day*
Past Yūsef zār '**i**mmo q**a**bᵉl sēᶜa — *Yusef visited his mother an hour ago.*
m**a**rati zārat '**u**mmi ('**i**mmi) — *My wife visited my mother.*

We can see that that zū- has turned into zā-.
In the same way, rūḥ *(go!)* → rāḥ *(he went)*
and jīb *(bring!)* → jāb *(he brought)*

What happens in the 1st and 2nd persons?

■
yā M**a**ryam, z**u**r-ti jirānek?	*Maryam, did you visit your neighbors?*
'**a**ywa, z**u**r-ᵉt jirāni	*Yes, I visited my neighbors.*
ya ulād, š**u**f-tu '**a**bu Yūsef?	*Hey kids, have you[pl] seen Abu Yusef?*
n**a**ᶜam, š**u**f-na '**a**bu Yūsef	*Yes, we've seen Abu Yusef.*
j**i**b-tu ḥalīb?	*Did you[pl] bring milk?*
'ā, j**i**b-na ḥalīb	*Yes, we've brought milk.*

You will have noticed that in the 1st and 2nd persons (*I, you[sing], we, you[pl]*, the long syllable becomes short:

zūr becomes z**u**r-
jīb becomes j**i**b-

In other words: **ū** shortens to **u** – **ī** shortens to **i**

Let's review all these forms by putting them in a table. Note that the 3rd person is, as always, the "odd man out," as its form is different from that of the 1st and 2nd persons:

z**u**rt	z**u**rt	z**u**rti			z**u**rna	z**u**rtu	
			zār	zārat			zāru
j**i**bt	j**i**bt	j**i**bti			j**i**bna	j**i**btu	
			jāb	jābat			jābu

Vocabulary

quṣṣɑ [quṣɑṣ]	story	kān	he was
ṣɑbi [ṣibyān]	boy, male child	kunt	I was
ђɑbɑr ['aђbɑ̄r]	information, news	fīʰ	there is, there are
il-bāqi	the rest, the remainder	ᶜindi	I've got, I have; at my house, by me
ḍēf [ḍyūf]	guest[m]	fīʰ ᶜindi	I've got, I have
qarīb (min)	near <from>	kān fīʰ	there was, there were
qarīb [qɑrɑ̄yeb]	relative, relation[m]	kān fīʰ ᶜindi	I had
ḥilu	sweet; beautiful, nice	or kān ᶜindi	I had
ṣɑ̄ḥeb [ṣḥɑ̄b]	friend; owner[m]	kān biddo[1]	he wanted
jōz / zawj[#]	husband	kunt biddi	I wanted

Conversation

– il-yōm iṣ-ṣubᵒḥ kunt	– I was at Umm Nabil's this morning <today the morning I was by Umm Nabil>.
ᶜind 'imm Nabīl[2], min zamān	I'd wanted to visit her for a long time
kunt biddi azūr-ha.	<from a long time I wanted….>
– šufᵉt jōz-ha kamān?	– Did you[m] see her husband, too?
– 'ɑ̄, šufto.	– Yes, I saw him.
– šū jibᵉt min hunāk?	– What did you bring [back] from there?
– jibᵉt ђɑbɑr!	– I brought news!
– in-šɑllɑ ђēr.	– Good news, I hope <if God wants, well>.
– 'aywa, 'imm Nabīl jābat[3] ṣɑbi.	– Yes, Umm Nabil has had <brought> a boy.
'abu Nabīl[2] mɑbṣūṭ!	Abu Nabil's delighted!
– hāda tāni[4] walad ᶜind-hom	– That's their second boy <… second boy by them>.
il-bāqi kull-hom banāt.	The rest are all <the rest all-of-them> girls.
ђamᵉs banāt fīʰ ᶜindhom.	They've got five girls.

---

1. Literally: *he was + he wants*. Likewise, kunt biddi = *I was + I want = I wanted.*

2. See **Lesson 9, Explanations 2**.

3. In colloquial Arabic *to give birth / to have a baby* is <to bring [into the world]>. If you inquire as to the whereabouts of a woman who has been taken to the maternity ward, you will be told rɑ̄ḥat‿etjīb = <She's gone to bring [a child into the world]>.

4. See below, **Explanations 1.**

– ya Jamīla, ru**ḥ**ti la-^{c}ind '**i**mm Nabīl? l**ā**zem‿^{e}tr**ū**ḥi!	– Jamila, did you go to [see] Umm Nabil? You've got to go!
– mà[5] z**u**rt-ha‿mb**ā**reḥ!	– But I visited her yesterday!
– š**ū** q**ā**lat?	– What did she say?
– q**ā**lat: '**a**hla u-s**a**hla!	– She said, "Welcome!"
– u-**i**nti, š**u** qultī-lha[6]?	– And you, what did you say to her?
– qult-**i**lha: mabr**ū**k!	– I said <I told her>, "Congratulations!"

– w**ē**n k**u**nt '**a**wwal‿^{e}mb**ē**reḥ[7]?	– Where were you^{m} the day before yesterday?
– ma k**u**nt-^{e}š fi-l-b**ē**t, k**u**nt fi ḥ**ē**fa.	– I wasn't at home, I was in Haifa.
– 'aђ**ū**y Fahīm š**ā**fak u-m**ɑ**rɑto kam**ā**n š**ā**fatak. h**i**yye kam**ā**n k**ā**nat fi ḥ**ē**fa. k**ā**nat b**i**d(d)-ha‿tz**ū**r‿^{e}ṣḥ**ɑ̄**b.	– My brother Fahim saw you, and his wife saw you, too. She was in Haifa as well. She wanted to visit friends.
– u-**i**ntu w**ē**n k**u**ntu fi n**a**fs il-w**a**qt?	– And you^{pl}, where were you at that time <at the same time>?
– mà[8] k**u**nna fi-l-b**ē**t!	– We were here at home, of course!

---

5. The word mà is unstressed (the stress falls on the verb that follows), it is not followed by -š, and it indicates a protest or a correction: *but* or *oh yes I / you /... they did!*

lēš ma jibt**ō**-š? *Why didn't you bring him / it?*
mà j**i**bto! *But I did bring him / it!*

You will find another example of this later on in the text.

6. Note that qultī-lha is followed immediately by qult-**i**lha. This will be explained in another lesson, later on.

7. *The day before yesterday* <first-yesterday>. Some people say 'aww**a**lt‿^{e}mb**ē**reḥ

8. See above footnote 5.

kān fīʰ ᶜin(d)na ḍyūf.	We had guests <there were at us guests>
– mīn hadōl lᵉ-ḍyūf (iḍ-ḍyūf) illi kānu ᶜin(d)-kom?	– Who were these guests who were at your place <by you>?
– nās min ᶜakka.	– People from Acco (Acre).
– ᵉṣḥāb?	– Friends?
– la', qarāyeb.	– No, relatives.
– 'abūk[9] kān mawjūd?	– Was your father there <... was present>?
– la', bass 'immi kānat mawjūde.	– No, but my mother was <present>.
'abūy rāḥ ᶜala nahariyya	My father went to Nahariyya
u-jāb‿ᵉmlabbas minšān iḍ-ḍyūf. ᶜašān l-ᵉḍyūf.	and brought sweets for the guests.

– wēn 'uẖtak?	– Where's yourᵐ sister?
– rāḥat ᶜa-s-sīnama.	– She's gone to the cinema.
– lēš ma ruḥt-ᵉš 'inte kamān?	– Why didn't you go too?
– il-filᵉm muš‿ᵉmnīḥ biddī-š ašūfo.	– It's not a good film <the f. [is] not good>. I don't want to see it.
– 'ana šufto, ktīr ḥilu kān.	– I saw it, it was very good.
maᶜalēš, marra tānye bᵉtrūḥ.	Never mind, you'll go another time <a second time you'll go>.
– šu biqūlu‿n-nās lamma bišūfu 'aflām[10] min ha-š-šikᵉl?	– What do people say when they see films of that kind?
– lamma šuft hal-filᵉm ana,	– For myself, when I saw that film <when I saw that film, I>
ᶜajab-ni[11] u-ᶜajab kull in-nās.	I liked it <it pleased me> and everyone [else] liked it <it pleased all the people>.

----

9. We've already seen that 'abu becomes 'abūy (*my father*). Here 'abu + -k becomes 'abūk. Explanations in the next lesson.

10. Yes, there are foreign words that have an Arabic plural form: filᵉm ['aflām] behaves like ẖabar ['aẖbār]. Galilean speakers, however, prefer the plural form [flūme]

11. The verb ᶜajab conjugates in the same way as katab. Why does the stress move from the first syllable of ᶜajab-ni to the second? We'll be learning that soon, too.

–'issa / halqēt ᶜindi quṣṣɑ ḥilwe.	– Now I've got a good <nice> story.
– qūl ta‿nšūf [12]!	– Let's hear it <tell, so that we see>!
– mɑrrɑ kān-fīʰ malek.	– Once there was a king.
kān ᶜindo 'ibᵉn 'aᶜma	He had a blind son
u-binᵉt ḫarsa…	and a dumb daughter.
– maskīn! balāš hal-quṣṣɑ!	– Poor thing! Not that story!
bid(d)na 'iši 'aḥla.	We want something nicer.
– ṭɑyyeb. mɑrrɑ kān-fīʰ malek.	– Fine. Once there was a king.
kān ᶜindo 'ibᵉn 'aḫras	He had a dumb son
u-bint ᶜamya…	and a blind daughter…
– bass, ya zalame, bass!	– Enough, man, enough!
fī-š ᶜindak ġēr hal-quṣɑṣ?	Don't you know any other stories <don't you have [anything] other than these stories>?

Explanations

1. tāni walad

In the conversation above we encountered the expression **tāni walad** (the second boy), which is another way of saying **il-walad it-tāni**, only in this case we omit the definite article il- and place the adjective **before** the noun. This expression is often used with the ordinal numbers and in sentences of the *this is / that is* type. Don't forget that the more usual form walad tāni means not only *a second boy* but also *another boy.* Note the differences:

■ mɑrrɑ tānye	*a second time / another time*
hāy tāni mɑrrɑ	*This is the second time*
mɑrrɑ tālte	*a third time*
tālet mɑrrɑ	*the third time*

When we look at the expressions **tāni mɑrrɑ** and **tālet mɑrrɑ** we notice something else. This unusual expression (it's unusual in that the adjective precedes the noun) is exceptional in another way, too: the adjective that precedes the noun stays **in the masculine** even when the noun is feminine. We say, for example:

■ hādi 'awwal mɑrrɑ — *This is the first time*

12. ta is a shortened form of ḥatta.

2. The comparative adjective (*more….. than*)

The comparative form of ḥ**i**lu is ’**a**ḥla. We’ll learn more about comparative adjectives in Lesson 15.

In the meantime, we’ll make do with the following examples:

	’**a**ḥla m**i**nnak	*more handsome than you*
	’**a**ḥla min h**ē**k	*nicer than that* <than thus>
■	ma f**i**šš ’**a**ḥla min h**ē**k	*There’s nothing nicer than that!*

That’ll do for time being.

3. ġ**ē**r = someone / something else; another… / different…

	ġ**ē**r hal-q**u**ṣɑṣ	*other stories* <something-else-other-than these stories>
	f**i**šš ġ**ē**r h**ā**da?	*Is there nothing else* <there isn’t [anything] other than this>?
	f**i**šš ġ**ē**ro?	*Isn’t there another one / a different one? Is there nobody else?*
	– ġ**ē**ro?	*Anything else?* (This is what shop assistants, etc., ask their customers)
■	’**i**nte ’**a**ḥsan min ġ**ē**rak?!	*Are you better than other people* <better than other-than-you>?

4. And finally…

We’ve seen that *in order to* in Arabic is ^{c}aš**ā**n, ḥ**a**tta, ta. You will also hear la- used in this sense, especially in the phrase: ta^{c}**ā**l la-aq**u**l-lak = *Come here, I’ve got something to tell you* <come that I tell you>.

This is such a commonly used phrase and it is said at such high speed that what
■ we usually hear is: t**a**^{c}-la-q**u**l-lak!

Exercises

A. Translate into English:

1. h**ā**di q**u**ṣṣɑ ḥ**i**lwe.
2. k**ī**f k**ā**n il-f**i**l^{e}m? ^{c}aj**a**b-kom?
3. h**ā**da f**i**lm‿^{e}jd**ī**d, bass ma ^{c}ajab-n**ī**-š.
4. q**a**b^{e}l j**u**m^{c}a š**u**fna f**i**l^{e}m ’**a**ḥla.
5. biq**ū**l kull y**ō**m nafs il-q**u**ṣṣɑ.
6. ^{c}**i**ndak qɑr**ɑ̄**yeb fil-q**u**ds?

7. l**a**’ bass fī^{h} ᶜ**i**ndi ṣḥ**ā**b‿^{e}kt**ī**r.
8. k**ā**nat b**i**dd-ha‿tz**ū**r ’**i**mm-ha (actually pronounced b**i**d-ha‿tz**ū**r ’**i**m-ha).

B. Complete the sentences:

9. j**i**b^{e}t ḥal**ī**b min (by / at) ’**i**mmi.
10. h**u**wwe z**ā**r-ni u-**a**na (I visited him).
11. biz**ū**r-ni kt**ī**r u-**a**na (visit him) kam**ā**n.
12. ya Y**ū**sef, š**ū** q**u**lt? ya M**a**ryam, (what did you say)?
13. r**ū**ḥ m**a**ᶜo (now).
14. ṣ**ā**ḥbak (did [he] go with you) ᶜa-s-s**ī**nama?
15. ’**a**ywa, ’**a**na (went) m**a**ᶜo ᶜa-s-s**ī**nama.
16. ’**i**mmi (went) maᶜ ’**u**ħti u-(saw) il-f**i**l^{e}m.
17. yā M**a**ryam, ᶜ**a**jabek il-f**i**l^{e}m?
18. ’**a**ywa, (I liked it^{m} <it pleased me>) kt**ī**r.

C. Translate into Arabic:

19. This is the fifth time he’s visited me <he visits me>.
20. What did he say to you^{m}?
21. He told me, “Go^{m} with him, I’ll go later.”
22. I’ve got relatives in Haifa.
23. And I’ve got friends in Acco.
24. Jamila, what did you tell the boy?
25. He brought sweets for <to> his sister.
26. You’re^{m} our guest.
27. You’re our guests.
28. My sister gave birth to <brought> a daughter.
29. My sister has a daughter <my sister, by her is a daughter>.
30. What more do you want <what do you want also>?

id-d**a**rs il-ḥ**ā**di ᶜ**ɑ**šɑr / d**a**rs‿iḥd**ɑ**ᶜš

11

The Eleventh Lesson / Lesson Eleven

We've already seen that the possessive pronouns added to the noun ’**a**bu (*father-of*) are slightly unusual: ’ab**ū**-y, ’ab**ū**-k (as opposed to b**ē**t-i b**ē**t-ak). Likewise, the pronouns attached to the preposition w**ɑ**rɑ *(behind)* differ from those used with the preposition minš**ā**n. Let's build up the paradigm

■ minš**ā**ni *for me*

wɑr**ɑ̄**y *behind me*

In the 2nd person singular, instead of -ak, -ek, we have -k, -ki:

minš**ā**n-ak	*for you*	minš**ā**n-ek	*for you*ᶠ
wɑr**ɑ̄**-k	*behind you*	wɑr**ɑ̄**-ki	*behind you*ᶠ

■ ya w**a**lad, w**ē**n ’ab**ū**-k? *Boy, where's your father?*

ya b**i**nᵉt, w**ē**n ’ab**ū**-ki? *Girl, where's your father?*

ya Y**ū**sef, il-k**u**rsi wɑr**ɑ̄**-k *Yusef, the chair's behind you.*

ya M**a**ryam, il-k**u**rsi wɑr**ɑ̄**-ki *Maryam, the chair's behind you.*

And in the 3rd person masculine singular

father-of	’**a**bu	→	’ab**ū**ʰ	*his father*
behind	w**ɑ**rɑ	→	wɑr**ɑ̄**ʰ	*behind him*

The final -h is not usually pronounced, but we can't omit it in transcription because it's going to be useful. In speech, the difference between *behind* and *behind him* lies in where **the stress** falls. When you listen to the recording, you'll notice that in those examples where the final -h is added, the stress moves to the last syllable of the word and the final vowel is lengthened slightly.

The same thing happens when you add an attached pronoun to any preposition or verb that **ends with a vowel**. For example:

They saw	š**ā**fu
They saw him/it	šāf**ū**ʰ
They see	biš**ū**fu
*They see you*ᶠ	bišūf**ū**-ki

Now we have all the information we need to tackle the text below and deal with a new set of problems. Don't worry, you'll soon see that they're not serious – and in fact there's really no problem at all!

Vocabulary

bustān	garden, orchard	ma… (-š) ḥada	[did] not anybody
ḥākūrɑ	yard, vegetable plot	bijūz	perhaps, possibly
kalb [klāb]	dog	'akl / 'akᵉl	food
zġīr [zġɑ̄r]	small; young	mɑyy	water
kbīr [kbɑ̄r]	big; adult; old	nāšef	dry
ḥādes [ḥawādes]	accident; event, incident		
ṣɑ̄r [iṣīr][1]	it happened / it occurred; he / it became		
il-ḥaqq ᶜala	is / are wrong <the right is on = against (somebody)>; (somebody) is to blame; it's (his / her / your / etc.) fault		

Conversation

– ya Nuha, il-jirɑ̄n šāfu 'aђū-ki?	– Nuha, did the neighbors see your brother?
– 'ɑ̄, šāfūʰ, kān fi-l-bustān.	– Yes, they did <they saw him>; he was in the garden.
– u-šāfū-ki kamān?	– And did they see you too?
– la'!	– No!
– ᵉmbala, 'Ilyās jɑ̄rna šāfek maᶜ 'aђūki, u-mɑrɑto kamān šāfatek. mà 'inti kunti maᶜ'aђūki fi-l-bustān.	– They did so! Elias, our neighbor, saw you with your brother, and his wife saw you, too. You **were** with your brother in the garden!
– 'ɑ̄, kunᵉt, bijūz šāfūni, lāken 'ana ma šuft-ᵉš ḥada.	– OK, I was. Perhaps they saw me but **I** didn't see anybody!
– ṭɑyyeb. wēn 'abū-ki u-immek?	– Fine. Where are your father and <your> mother?
– 'abṣɑr[2]. sa'alt 'Aḥmad 'aђūy?	– I don't know. Did you ask my brother Ahmad?

---

1. Remember that for verbs the form in square brackets is the subjunctive. This verb is conjugated like jāb [ijīb].
2. 'abṣɑr is not a verb, but an adjective. It means *more clear-sighted.* In other words, *I don't know, but there is someone who is more clear-sighted than me* (i.e., Allah).

– ’**a**ywa, sa’**a**lto. qult-**i**llo:	– Yes, I did <I asked him>. I said to him:
“w**ē**n ’ab**ū**k u-**i**mmak?”	“Where are your father and mother?”
q**a**l-li: q**a**b^{e}l s**ē**^{c}a k**ā**nu	He told me: “An hour ago <before an hour>
fi-l-b**ē**t. ’**i**ssa / h**a**llaq	they were at home. I don’t know
’**a**bṣɑr w**ē**n r**ɑ̄**ḥu.	where they’ve gone now.”

– ya ul**ā**d, j**i**btu‿l-k**a**lb	– Kids, did you bring the little
l-^{e}zġ**ī**r illi k**ā**n fi-l-ḥāk**ū**rɑ?	dog that was in the yard?
– ’**a**ywa, u-jibn**ā**-lo kam**ā**n ’**a**k^{e}l.	– Yes, and we brought him food, too.
bass ma bidd**ō**-š hal-’**a**k^{e}l!	But he doesn’t want that food.
– il-ḥ**a**qq ^{c}ala m**ī**n?	– Whose fault is that?
– il-ḥ**a**qq ^{c}al**ē**^{h}, hal-’**a**k^{e}l	– It’s his fault. That food’s
ṭɑyyeb‿^{e}kt**ī**r.	very good.
– **la**’, il-ḥ**a**qq ^{c}al**ē**-ki, ya b**i**nt.	– No, it’s your fault, girl,
li’**a**nno h**ā**da n**ā**šef.	because it’s <that’s> dry.
j**ī**bi m**ɑ**yy u-b^{e}tš**ū**fi šu biṣ**ī**r.	Bring [some] water and you’ll see what happens.
(j**ā**bat m**ɑ**yy: il-k**a**lb	(She brought water and the dog
’**a**kal il-k**u**ll.)	ate everything <ate the-all>.)

– š**ū** ṣ**ɑ̄**r?	– What’s up?
– w**a**la ’**i**ši!	– Nothing <and not a thing>!
– ^{e}mb**a**la! ṣ**ɑ̄**r ma^{c}o ḥ**ā**des,	– Come on! He had an accident <happened with him an accident>.
k**ā**n majr**ū**ḥ, ’aђad**ū**^{h}	He was hurt, they took him
^{c}a-l-must**a**šfa, u-…	to hospital, and...
’**i**ssa/halq**ē**t jāb**ū**^{h} ^{c}a-l-b**ē**t.	now they’ve brought him home.
– ṣ**ɑ̄**r ’**a**ḥsan, y**a**^{c}ni?	– So he’s better <he’s become better, it means>?
– ’**ɑ̄**, ђɑlɑṣ, bass k**u**ll il-q**u**ṣṣɑ	– Yes, it’s over <finished>, but the whole thing
’**a**ђdat[3] m**a**^{c}na t**a**lat sē^{c}**ā**t.	<all the story> took us three hours.

3. Note the expression **’aђad** m**a**^{c}i s**ē**^{c}a = *it took me* <with me> *an hour.* qadd**ē**š ’**a**ђad m**a**^{c}ak (w**a**q^{e}t)? = *How long did it take you* <how much did it take with you time>?

Explanations

1. Pronouns

We know that when a verb ends in a vowel – e.g., z**ā**ru, kat**a**bti – the final vowel is unstressed, so when you **do** hear a stressed (and lengthened) final vowel it's a sure sign that a pronoun (*he, it*) has been attached to the verb:

they visit	biz**ū**ru	pronounced	bi **zū** ru
*they visit **him***	bizūr**ū**^{h}	pronounced	bi zū **rū**^{h} _ _↗

■ – Ya **b**int, jībi‿l-k**a**lb. – *Girl, bring the dog!*
– š**ū**? ajīb[4] il-k**a**lb la-h**ō**n? – *What? Bring the dog here <to here>?*
– '**a**ywa, jīb**ī**^{h} la-h**ō**n. – *Yes, bring it here!*

– b^{e}tš**ū**fi 'aђ**ū**ki b**u**krα? – *Will you see your brother tomorrow?*
– y**i**mken. – *Perhaps.*
– '**i**za b^{e}tšūf**ī**^{h}, qul**ī**-lo b**i**ddi az**ū**ro. – *If you see him, tell him I want to visit him.*

Note: baz**ū**r / b^{e}tz**ū**ri = I visit / you^{f} visit
baz**ū**r-o / b^{e}tzūr**ī**^{h} = I visit him / you^{f} visit him

The two different forms of the attached pronouns are summarized in the table opposite. Remember, the form used depends on the answer to the question: "Does the word end in a consonant or a vowel?"

---

4. aj**ī**b = *should I bring?* or *that I bring?* (subjunctive, i.e., without the prefix b-).
Another example: ar**ū**ḥ ma^{c}ak? means *[Do you want] me to go with you?*

Words ending in a consonant	**Words ending in a vowel (-a, -i, -u)**
quddām = *in front of*	wara = *behind*
quddā**m**-i	war**ā**-y
quddā**m**-ak	war**ā**-k
quddā**m**-ek	war**ā**-ki
quddā**m**-o	war**ā**ʰ
quddā**m**-ha =	war**ā**-ha
quddā**m**-na	war**ā**-na
quddā**m**-kom (-ku)	war**ā**-kom (-ku)
quddā**m**-hom (-hen)	war**ā**-hom (-hen)

Let's sum up what we've learned so far:

– When a word ends in a / i / u, the final vowel is short and the syllable is unstressed.

– But when we add any kind of suffix, such as the negative particle -š, or an attached pronoun, or l- + an attached pronoun (-li, -lak, -lo), the final syllable is stressed and lengthened.

If you are not too keen on theory and rules, just repeat ***out loud*** *the examples in the box below, and you'll absorb the rule naturally.*

they brought		you$^{f\ sing}$ brought	
j**ā**bu	ma jāb**ū**-š	j**i**bti	ma jibt**ī**-š
j**ā**bu	jāb**ū**-ha	j**i**bti	jibt**ī**-ha
j**ā**bu	jāb**ū**-li	j**i**bti	jibt**ī**-li

2. On me, on you…

This is a good place to review the whole paradigm of the preposition ᶜ**a**la / ᶜala (*on, at*) with its attached pronouns. Note that when used with these pronouns, ᶜala behaves as if it were ᶜal**ē**-:

ᶜal**a**yy/ᶜal**a**yyi (-yye) ᶜal**ē**-k ᶜal**ē**-ki ᶜal**ē**ʰ ᶜal**ē**-ha

ᶜal**ē**-na ᶜal**ē**-kom / -ku ᶜal**ē**-hom (-hen)

Now we can understand the expression ma ᶜal**ē**-š (*it doesn't matter*). It's a shortened form of ma ᶜal**ē**ʰ ši = *there is not on it / about it a thing*, in other words, *there's nothing to say, there's no problem / objection.*

3. Here is / here's / here are = h**a**yy-o [J] // hayy**ā**^{h} or hiyy**ā**^{h} [G]

This also helps us to understand the pronunciation of the two forms (used in Jerusalem and Galilee) of the word that means *here is / here are*:

here he is h**a**yy-o // hiyy**ā**^{h}
here she is h**a**yy-ha // hiyy**ā**-ha

Note that in the first person singular the suffix is the one used with verbs, -ni:
here I am h**a**yy-ni // hiyy**ā** -ni

A quick exercise:

How do you reply to the following questions?
For example:
1. š**u**f^{e}t 'aħ**ū**k? – '**a**ywa, š**u**fto

Continue:
2. ya n**ā**s, š**u**ftu 'aħ**ū**y? – '**a**ywa, …
3. il-jir**ɑ̄**n š**ā**fu b**i**ntak? – '**a**ywa, …
4. in-n**ā**s b**i**d-hom iš**ū**fu‿l-f**i**l^{e}m? – '**a**ywa, b**i**dhom…
5. '**i**mmak š**ā**fat il-k**a**lb? – '**a**ywa, …
6. j**i**btu‿l-jar**ī**de? – '**a**ywa, …
7. f**ī**^{h} n**ā**s wɑr**ɑ̄**y? – '**a**ywa, f**ī**^{h} n**ā**s[5]...
8. l**ā**zem aj**ī**b il-b**i**nt? – '**a**ywa,…
9. l**ā**zem‿^{e}nz**ū**r il-m**a**tḥaf[6]? – '**a**ywa, l**ā**zem‿^{e}t-… '**i**ntu kam**ā**n.
10. il-ḥ**a**qq ^{c}ala‿l-jir**ɑ̄**n? – '**a**ywa, il-ḥ**a**qq …
11. il-ḥ**a**qq ^{c}al**ē**ha! – l**a**', il-ḥ**a**qq (the right is against you, = you are wrong)
12. il-ul**ā**d k**a**tabu‿d-d**a**rs? – '**a**ywa, ka-…
13. u-**i**nte kam**ā**n kat**a**bt id-d**a**rs? – '**a**ywa, ka-…

4. Who, which, that

A useful tool for doing the exercises will be the word illi, which means *who, which, that*. Let's look at the following phrases:

■ kat**a**bt il-makt**ū**b *I wrote the letter*
il-makt**ū**b illi kat**a**bt-o *the letter **that** I wrote* <it>

---

5. There are two possible answers, depending on who's asking (male or female).

6. m**a**tḥaf = *museum.* t**u**ḥfe [t**u**ḥaf] = *work of art* or *masterpiece*; the m**a**tḥaf is the place for t**u**ḥaf. Marvelling at a beautiful object, people say: t**u**ḥfe! / š**ū** hat-t**u**ḥfe! = *How beautiful* < what [is] this tuhfe>!

Note that while in English we can say "the letter which / that I wrote" or "the letter I wrote," in Arabic there is no alternative but to say "the letter **which / that** I wrote **it.**"

■ daf**a**^{c}t hal-m**a**blaġ	*You paid that amount*
hal-m**a**blaġ illi daf**a**^{c}t-o	*That amount which you paid* <it>
š**ā**f il-m**a**drase	*He saw the school*
il-m**a**drase illi š**ā**f-ha	*The school that he saw* <it>
j**i**bna‿l-muft**ā**ḥ	*We've brought the key*
il-muft**ā**ḥ illi jibn**ā**^{h}	*The key that we've brought* <it>

You can see now that by playing around with verbs and simple phrases you can turn them into sentences using illi. This will allow you to practice adding the attached pronouns to verbs. For example:

š**u**fna hal-w**a**lad fi-š-š**ā**re^{c}	*We saw that boy in the street*
il-w**a**lad illi …[7] fi-s-s**ā**re^{c}	*The boy whom / that we saw in the street.*

Last exercise

Read out loud:	and say out loud in Arabic:
14. š**u**fna hal-b**i**nt fi-l-m**a**drase	*The girl we saw at the school*
15. daf**a**^{c}na‿l-m**a**blaġ‿^{e}mb**ē**reḥ	*The sum we paid yesterday*
16. z**u**rna‿l-m**a**drase	*The school that we visited* <it^{f}>
17. j**i**bti‿l-jar**ī**de?	*The newspaper that you brought*
18. b**i**ntak š**ā**fat il-f**i**l^{e}m	*The film that she saw*

'**i**ntu ta^{c}bānīn? ma^{c}alēš - It was worth it! We've taken a big step forward today. Let's be content with that, and dispense with any further exercises…

Well, perhaps just one more…

My mother and <my> father, your mother and <your> father, etc.:

'ab**ū**y u-**i**mmi	'ab**ū**-k u-**i**mm-ak	'ab**ū**-ki u-**i**mm-ek
'ab**ū**^{h} u-**i**mmo	'ab**ū**-ha u-**i**m-ha	
'ab**ū**-na u-**i**m-na*	'ab**ū**-kom u-**i**m-kom*	'ab**ū**-hom u-**i**m-hom*

----

* We don't hear the doubling of the consonant -m- when it is not followed by a vowel (see **Lesson 6, Explanations 1,** and p. 110, Doubled consonants.

7. .. *we saw him* = šufn**ā**^{h}. Did you work it out? Well done!

id-dars it̠-t̠āni ᶜ**ɑ**šɑr[1] – dars‿etn**ɑ**ᶜeš

12

The Twelfth Lesson (Lesson Twelve)

We're going to take another step forward, even though you won't yet have absorbed everything you've learned so far: today we'll be looking at the present-future (and the subjunctive) of verbs like k**a**tab.

■ b**u**krɑ b**i**ddi **a**kteb la-'**i**mmi	*Tomorrow I want to write to my mother*
h**ē**k b-**a**kteb '**i**smi	*That's how I write my name* <thus I write>
b**i**ddi **a**dros id-d**a**rs	*I want to study the lesson*
kull y**ō**m b-**a**dros id-d**a**rs	*Every day I study the lesson*
hal-m**ɑ**rrɑ ma bidd**ī**-š '**a**dfaᶜ	*This time I don't want to pay*
bass ᶜ**ā**datan b-**a**dfaᶜ	*but usually I pay*

Arabic verbs of this kind assume one of three possible forms:

'**a**drOs '**a**kteb '**a**dfaᶜ

Elephant in Arabic is fīl

In the texts that follow you'll be able to observe the conjugation of each form, and you will most certainly recognize the prefixes and suffixes with which you are familiar from the conjugation of the verb š**ū**f: 'a-š**ū**f, ᵉn-š**ū**f, ᵉt-š**ū**f-u.

In this lesson we'll learn only verbs that have the pattern **ba**□□a̲□ in the present-future tense, i.e., those that have *a* as their second vowel. In Lesson 13 we'll meet verbs from the patterns **ba**□□e□, **ba**□□o□.

---

1. This is how you say *twelfth* in literary Arabic – hence the t̠- (see page [11]). In colloquial Arabic this letter usually turns into t- (t**ā**ni).

Vocabulary[2]

ba^{c}at	he sent	**da**fa^{c}	he paid
'**ab**^{c}at	that I send (subj.)	'**ad**fa^{c}	that I pay
fatah̩[3]	he opened	**za**ra^{c}	he sowed
'**a**ftaḥ	that I open	'**az**ra^{c}	that I sow
m**a**na^{c}	he prevented / forbade	**sa**'al	he asked
'**a**mna^{c}	that I prevent	'**as**'al	that I ask
^{c}**ā**de [^{c}ād**ā**t]	custom, habit	^{c}**ā**datan	usually, normally
šubb**ā**k [šabābīk]	window	'**ɑ**rḍ ['ɑr**ɑ̄**ḍi]	land, plot, field
fall**ā**ḥ [fallāḥ**ī**n]	farmer, *fellah*	jaw**ā**b	answer, reply

Conversation

– ba^{c}**a**tna makt**ū**b la-mud**ī**r il-m**a**drase, f**i**šš jaw**ā**b. – We sent a letter to the headmaster of the school, [but] he hasn't replied <there's no reply>.

– l**ā**zem t**i**b^{c}atu makt**ū**b t**ā**ni. – You[pl] must sent another letter.

– '**ɑ̄**, b**i**dna n**i**b^{c}at kam**ā**n makt**ū**b u-b^{e}nš**ū**f //m^{e}nš**ū**f š**ū** b**i**ṣ**ī**r. – Yes, we're going to send another letter, and we'll see what happens.

– l**ē**š fat**a**ḥti‿š-šabāb**ī**k? muš l**ā**zem t**i**ftaḥi halq**ē**t. – Why have you[f] opened the windows? There's no need for you to open them now <it must not that you open now>.

– d**ā**yman b**a**ftaḥ iṣ-ṣ**u**b^{o}ḥ‿^{e}šw**a**yy, u-'**i**ssa b**i**ddi **a**ftaḥ bass r**u**b^{ec} s**ē**^{c}a. – I always open [them] a bit in the morning, and now I want to open [them] just [for] a quarter of an hour.

– muš l**ā**zem n**i**ftaḥ šubbāk**ē**n, šubb**ā**k w**ā**ḥad bik**a**ffi. 'iza bn**i**ftaḥ šubbāk**ē**n, – We don't need to open two windows, one window's enough. If we open two windows there'll

---

2. This vocabulary list (which, as usual, contains only a few new key words used in the text; the rest can be understood with the help of the translation) includes verbs that take -a in the subjunctive / present-future tense, e.g., t**i**ftaḥ. There is a reason for this.

3. We have already encountered the root f-t-ḥ in the word muft**ā**ḥ.

bikūn fīʰ majrα hawa[5].	be <[it] will-be there-is> a draft.
– ṭαyyeb, qūl lal-walad	– OK, tell[m] the boy to open the window
yiftaḥ iš-šubbāk illi ḥadd il-bāb	beside the door <that he open the window that [is] beside…>
u-ma yiftaḥ šubbāk tāni.	and not to open another window.

(A conversation with a *fellah*)

– marḥaba[6].	– Hello.
– 'ahlan!	– Hello.
– la-wēn? šu šuġlak il-yōm?	– Where are you going <to where>? What are you doing <what's your work> today?
– bidna nizraᶜ duḫḫān.[7]	– We're going to sow tobacco.
– wēn‿ᵉbtizraᶜu‿d-duḫḫān?	– Where will you sow the tobacco?
– ᶜin(d)na 'αrḍ jamb il-bēt.	– We've got [a plot of] land beside the house.
il-ᶜām[8] zaraᶜna kūsa,	Last year we sowed courgettes / zucchini,
has-sane bnizraᶜ duḫḫān	this year we're sowing tobacco
u-bᵉnšūf.[9]	and we'll see [what happens].
– ᵉmbayyen has-sane kull fallāḥīn	– It seems that this year all the village
il-balad bidhom yizraᶜu duḫḫān.	farmers want to sow tobacco.
bass ᶜin(d)kom ᶜādatan	But you don't usually sow tobacco
bizraᶜū-š duḫḫān.	<by you (pl) usually [they] don't sow…>.

---

5. majrα means *current*. Its plural form, majāri, means *sewage [system]*; hawa means *air, wind.* il-yōm fīʰ hawa = *It's windy today* <today there's wind>.

6. The expression marḥaba (or marḥαbα) is used to greet people we meet outside the home (ours or theirs), in the course of the day . The root r-ḥ-b expresses the idea of *space*, (in literary Arabic raḥba = *[a] public square*). The proper response to marḥαbα is 'ahlan, or marḥabtēn (twice marḥaba).

7. The word duḫḫān literally means *smoke* – so farmers who plant tobacco are sowing a crop that turns into smoke and is borne away by the wind.

8. ᶜām means *year*; the word *last* has been omitted here. You could also say is-sine‿l-mᾱḍye (this expression will be explained later)

9. In Galilee sine, mnizraᶜ, mᵉnšūf (in Jerusalem: sane/sana, bnizraᶜ, bᵉnšūf).

ᶜala kull ḥ**ā**l, ’**α**llα‿iw**a**ffeq[10]!	Good luck, anyway <in any case, may God cause you to succeed>!
– ’**α**llα yiḥfαẓαk.	– Thanks <may God preserve you>.

– biq**ū**lu inno l**ā**zem n**i**dfaᶜ ḍαr**ī**be ᶜala k**u**ll ’**i**ši.	– They say we’ve got to pay tax on everything.
– ’**ᾱ**, kull in-n**ā**s bʸ**i**dfaᶜu[11] ḍαr**ᾱ**yeb. muš m**u**mken n**i**mnaᶜ h**ā**da!	– Yes, everyone pays taxes. We can’t do anything about it <it’s impossible that we prevent it>!
– ’**a**ywa, h**ā**da ’**i**ši muš m**u**mken n**i**mnaᶜo.	– Yes, that’s something we can’t do anything about.
– qadd**ē**š daf**a**ᶜet la-ḥadd ’**i**ssa, u-qadd**ē**š l**ā**zem t**i**dfaᶜ kam**ā**n?	– How much have youᵐ paid so far <until now>, and how much do you still <also> have to pay?
– daf**a**ᶜet ḫams**ī**n š**ē**kel u-b**a**ᶜᵉd[12] // l**i**ssa l**ā**zem ’**a**dfaᶜ ḫ**a**mse u-ᶜišr**ī**n.	– I’ve paid fifty shekels, and I’ve still got to pay <and still I must…> twenty-five.
– u-**i**nti, qadd**ē**š daf**a**ᶜti u-qadd**ē**š l**ā**zem t**i**dfaᶜi?	– And youᶠ, how much have you paid and how much do you have to pay?
– n**a**fs‿iš-š**i**.	– The same thing.
– k**ā**n l**ā**zem t**i**dfaᶜi ’**a**ktαr m**i**nni ᶜaš**ā**n ᶜ**i**ndek b**ē**t ’**a**kbαr min b**ē**ti.	– Youᶠ should have to pay more than me, <[it] was necessary that you pay> you’ve got a house [that’s] bigger than mine.
– ᶜala kull ḥ**ā**l b**a**dfaᶜ hal-m**a**blaġ kull š**a**hᵉr u-bik**a**ffi. miš l**ā**zem n**i**s’al‿ekt**ī**r… ’**a**na ma bas’**a**l-ᵉš!	– In any case, I pay this sum every month and that’s enough. We mustn’t ask a lot of questions. [As for me] I don’t ask.
– mαẓb**ū**ṭ, muš l**ā**zem t**i**s’ali.	– That’s right, you shouldn’t ask.

---

10. This verb form will be explained later on.
11. See below, **Explanations 1**, footnote 13.
12. See below, **Explanations 3.**

Explanations

1. Prefixes for the verb in the present-future tense

We have seen that the prefixes in the subjunctive of **šūf** / **jīb** are:

a- / t- (et-) / i- / n- (en-)

The subjunctive of verbs like **fataḥ**, **dafa**ᶜ, on the other hand, begins with two consonants with no intervening vowel: **-ftaḥ**, **-dfa**ᶜ. With verbs like these, the prefixes t- and n- add a helping i:

t- → ti-, n- → ni-.

With the b- of the present-future these prefixes become: bti- and bni-.

Let's compare the two families and get used to this minor difference:

■	*I open*	b**a**-ftaḥ	ba-š**ū**f	*I see*
	you^{ms} *open*	bt**i**-ftaḥ	bᵉt-š**ū**f	*you see*
	he opens	bʸ**i**-ftaḥ[13]	bi-š**ū**f	*he sees*
	we open	bn**i**-ftaḥ	bᵉn-š**ū**f	*we see*
		[mn**i**-ftaḥ	mᵉn-š**ū**f]^{G}	

Don't worry! As you listen to the texts (and read them out loud) all this will become automatic and the correct form will occur to you spontaneously. This means that you have learned **the prefixes to all the possible forms of the verb**: you will see this confirmed each time we come across a new type of verb.

2. The negative particle -š

When we add the negative particle -š the stress usually moves to the last syllable of the word:

■	*I ask*	b**a**s'al	ma bas'**a**l-ᵉš	*I don't ask*
	you^{pl} *sow*	bt**i**zraᶜu	ma btizraᶜ**ū**-š	*you don't sow*
	you^{m} *ask him*	bt**i**s'alo	ma btis'al**ō**-š	*you don't ask him*

---

13. Most people pronounce this as **bi-ftaḥ**. In the subjunctive, however (where the prefix b- is absent) the y- is clearly heard: **lāzem yi-ftaḥ** = *he must open.*

If you'd rather not use -š, you can just use ma on its own; if you do this, the position of the stress doesn't change: **mā** ba**s**'al. = *I don't ask.*

The use of ma on its own is characteristic of a higher register of speech, and is less commonly heard.

> **Why is it so important to get the stress in the right place?**
> *(Read this at your leisure, when you're in a relaxed frame of mind)*
> - Stress is not a particularly complex issue, and you will gradually acquire the habit of emphasizing words in the proper place. However, we want to draw your attention to it at an early stage, as an understanding and awareness of the importance of stress will enable you to apply the rules that govern it (which are few, and not difficult at all!)
> - **Stress is very important indeed!** If you don't stress words in the right places you'll find it hard to speak fluently, especially when using long sentences. What's more, the people you talk to are liable to misunderstand you, because **misplaced stress can, in some cases, change the meaning of an entire sentence!** We'll provide examples of this later on.
> - It's worth while learning how to stress words properly from the outset: it'll stand you in good stead in the future.

A short exercise:

Translate into Arabic and read out loud:

1. You^{f} must open <[it is] necessary [that] you open>.
2. I want to pay; I pay.
3. I'll pay this sum <this sum, I'll pay it>.
4. He's got to ask <[it is] necessary [that] he ask>.
5. He asks the boss.
6. He asks him.

3. Yet, still / not yet

The words **li**ssa^{J} and **ba**^{c}d / **ba**^{c}ed^{G} mean *still* and *not yet / hasn't..... yet.* We won't go over all the possible usages of these words at this point, but let's look at a few examples and try to remember:

ba^{c}ed **fī**^{h} // **li**ssa **fī**^{h}	*there's still*
ba^{c}ed-ni // lis**sā**-ni	*I'm still*
ba^{c}d-ak // lis**sā**k	*you$^{m\ sing}$ are still*

– With a verb in a negative sentence:

■ baᶜed-ni ma ruḥt-ᵉš [G] — *I haven't gone yet.*

lissa (lissāni) ma ruḥt-ᵉš

baᶜdo ma dafaᶜ-ᵉš [G] — *He still hasn't paid.*

lissa ma dafaᶜ-š

– In response to a question:

– dafaᶜet? / ma dafaᶜt-ᵉš? — *– Have you[m] paid? / Haven't you paid?*

– lissa // baᶜed. — *– Not yet.*

The word lissa can take another form, too: **lissāt-**. This form is used only with the attached personal pronouns. This means we have two alternative paradigms:

lissā-ni lissā-k lissā-ki lissāʰ lissā-ha lissā-na, -kom, -hom

lissāt-ni lissāt-ak lissāt-ek lissāt-o lissāt-ha lissāt-na, -kom, -hom

Exercise

How do you say (in Galilee or Jerusalem, depending on where you live):

7. Are you[m] still here?!
8. Are you[f] still here?!
9. They're still[14] at the museum.
10. They haven't opened yet.
11. I still live in the same house.

And perhaps il-yōm… bikaffi!

If you like, you can put off the exercises until another day. Then tomorrow you can go back over Lesson 12 and the **Explanations**. Afterwards you can do the following exercises:

Exercises

A. Translate into English:

12. mnibᶜat // bnibᶜat hal-maktūb?

 'ā, mnibᶜato; la', ma mnibᶜatō-š.

13. yā Samīrα, sa'alti‿l-mudīr?
14. lēš ma sa'altī-š il-mudīr.
15. lāzem tis'alīʰ.

---

14. It's best to avoid hybrids that mix the characteristics of Jerusalem and Galilee speech, such as baᶜed-hom (!) *(they still are...)*, which you may occasionally come across in language manuals for foreigners. On the whole, people who say baᶜed use the ending -hen, while those who say -hom use the word lissa (Jerusalem). So you should say either baᶜed-hen or lissā-hom.

16. ’**i**za b**i**ddi **a**ftaḥ, b**a**ftaḥ.
17. b**i**ddi **a**ftaḥ il-b**ā**b; h**a**llaq b**a**ftaḥo.
18. muš l**ā**zem t**i**ftaḥ. l**ē**š‿ᵉbt**i**ftaḥ?
19. bi-’**ē**š *(= with what)* b**i**ddak t**i**ftaḥ? – b**i**ddi **a**ftaḥ bil-muft**ā**ḥ.

B. Complete the sentences

(Replace the English words with the appropriate expression in Arabic):

20. il-m**a**blaġ **i**lli (I paid <it>)
21. muš l**ā**zem (to pay) <that you^{m} pay> h**a**llaq.
22. sa’**a**lt ’ab**ū**k? – Not yet.
23. (Usually) b**a**ftaḥ il-b**ā**b ḥ**a**tta if**ū**t, (=in order that he come in)…
24. …bass hal-m**a**rra (I don’t want to open).
25. il-makt**ū**b **i**lli (you^{pl} wrote <it>).
26. il-b**ā**b **i**lli (I / we opened <it>).

C. Translate into Arabic:

27. Every day he opens the windows.
28. Does he open the door? – Yes, he opens it. – No, he doesn’t open it.
29. Who asked you$^{m/f}$? – He’s got to ask his mother.
30. You^{m} don’t have to ask / You mustn’t ask <it’s not necessary that you ask>.

id-**d**ars it-**t**ālet ᶜ**α**šαr – **d**ars talatt**α**ᶜeš

13

The Thirteenth Lesson (Lesson Thirteen)

The new verbs we encountered in the last lesson, such as **fa**taḥ, **ba**ᶜat, and **sa**'al, all follow the pattern **ba**□□a□ in the present-future tense, i.e., they have *a* as their second vowel, e.g., **ba**ftaḥ (*I open).* Let's take a look at some verbs with a different second vowel in the present-future and subjunctive:

t**a**rak *he left*	'**a**tr**e**k *that I leave*	**ba**tr**e**k *I leave / I'll leave*
s**a**kat *he was silent*	'**a**sk**o**t *that I be silent*	**ba**sk**o**t *I'm silent / I'll be silent*

If the second vowel is *e*, the prefixes that denote *you, he/she* and *we* will be t**i**-, y**i**-, n**i**-, just as they are in verbs that have *a* as their second vowel, e.g.,

l**ā**zem *it's necessary*	t**i**trek *that you leave*	y**i**trek *that he leave*	n**i**trek *that we leave*

We'll pause the conjugation here for the time being.

(Are you wondering about *you* $^{\text{f and pl}}$ *leave* and *they leave*? You'll find out about them in Lesson 17.)

If, however, the second vowel in the present-future tense is *o* ('**a**skot), the prefixes will be tu-, yu-, nu-. This happens because the vowel of the prefix “identifies with” the second vowel (*o* and *u* are phonetically close) and imitates its sound: **tu**skot *that you*[m] *be silent*, **yu**skot[1] *that he be silent.*

Sometimes the pronunciation of the vowels of a particular verb varies from one area to another. For example, although you will normally hear the form **ti**kteb, **yi**kteb, you may also hear people say **tu**ktob, **yu**ktob.

As usual, we’ll dive straight into the next text – that’s the best way to learn to swim!

Vocabulary

rαbαṭ [**yu**rboṭ]	to tie[2] (up) / attach	qal**ī**l	a little
ġasal [**yi**ġsel]	to wash / do laundry	ġas**ī**l	washing, laundry
samaḥ [**yi**smaḥ]	to allow / permit	’**a**ḥsan	better
ṭαlαb [**yu**ṭlob]	to ask for / request	’**a**ḥsan-ma	so that (I, you…won’t)
ḫabaz [**yi**ḫbez]	to bake (bread)	ḫαṭαr	danger
ḥαṣαd [**yu**ḥṣod]	to harvest / reap	f**ē**n (=w**ē**n)	where (in s.a.)
ḍαrαb [**yu**ḍrob]	to hit	ᶜa-l-qal**ī**le	at least
hαrαb [**yu**hrob]	to run away / escape	ᶜ**a**jan [**yi**ᶜjen]	to knead (dough)
našαr [**yu**nšor]	to hang out (laundry); to publish		
z**ō**baᶜa [zaw**ā**beᶜ]	storm		

Conversation

– **bi**dna **nu**ktob / **ni**kteb makt**ū**b lal-mud**ī**r;’**i**za ma mnukt**o**b-š hal-makt**ū**b, muš **mu**mken **ni**bᶜato! – We want to write a letter to the manager; if we don’t write the <this> letter, we won’t be able to send it <not possible that we send it>!

– **bi**ddi **ar**boṭ hal-ḥ**a**bᵉl. – I want to tie that rope.

– l**ē**š‿ᵉbt**u**rboṭ il-h**a**bᵉl h**ē**k? – Why are you tying the rope like that <thus>?

---

1. With the prefix b-: by**u**skot (*he is silent*), but more often the y is not heard: bʸ**u**skot → b**u**skot. See footnote 13, p.80.

2. Until now we have introduced each new verb by its 3rd person masculine singular, considered the basic verbal form in Arabic: **ka**tab = *he wrote*. From now on we'll add the subjunctive and use the English infinitive to translate the pair: **ka**tab [**yi**kteb] = to write.

– ma rɑbɑṭṭū-š[3] il-kalb?	– Didn't you tie up the dog?
– ^{e}mbala, rɑbɑṭna‿l-kalb fil-bēt.	– Yes we did, we tied the dog up in the house.
– 'aywa, rɑbɑṭnā^{h}	– Yes, we tied it up
'aḥsan-ma[4] yuhrob.	so it wouldn't run away.
dāyman b^{y}uhrob min il-bēt	It always runs away from home
u-fī^{h} ђɑṭɑr ^{c}alē^{h}.	and it's dangerous for it <there is danger on it>.
– ^{e}mbēreḥ hɑrɑb, bass il-yōm	– It ran away yesterday, but today
muš mumken yuhrob,	it can't run away
li'anno mɑrbūṭ[5].	because it's tied up.

– mɑrɑti ġaslat u-našrat il-ġasīl,	– My wife did laundry and hung out the washing,
u-ba^{c}dēn ^{c}ajnat u-ђabzat.	then she kneaded dough and baked bread.
– kull yōm‿^{e}btiġsel u-btunšor	– Does she do laundry, hang out the washing,
il-ġasīl u-bti^{c}jen u-btiђbez?	knead dough and bake bread every day?
– la', bass kull tlatt‿iyyām,	– No, only every three days,
hēk taqrīban.	more or less <thus nearly>.

ġasīl, ġasīl, ġasīl, ġasīl, ġasīl, ġasīl, ġasīl,…

---

3. rɑbɑṭṭu is usually pronounced rɑbɑṭṭu (the t is assimilated into the ṭ).
4. Literally *better than ...; (he did that) so that (something) wouldn't happen* <better than that (something) will happen>.
5. li'ann-o = *because he / it...* mɑrbūṭ = *tied up, attached.* We'll revisit this later.

– šu btuṭlob fi maktūbak?	– What are you asking for in your letter?
– baṭlob maṣāri, lāzem yidfa^{c}!	– I'm asking for money, he's got to pay!
lāzem yidfa^{c}-li ^{c}a-l-qalīle	He's got to pay me at least twenty shekels,
^{c}išrīn šēkel, baṭlob-š 'aktar.	I'm not asking for [any] more.

– hal-walad dāyman b^{y}uḍrob	– That boy is always hitting his sister
'uḫto u-hiyye btuskot.	but <and> she doesn't say anything.
– ba^{c}dēn 'immi btuḍrob il-walad…	– Then my mother hits the boy …
– u-huwwe kamān b^{y}uskot?	– And does he keep quiet, too?
– la'! huwwe ma buskot-š!	– No! **He** doesn't keep quiet!

(fi-l-maktab:)	(At the office:)
– law samaḥti[6], fēn il-mudīr?	– Excuse me, where's the manager?
– kān hōn qab^{e}l sē^{c}a u-rāḥ.	– He was here an hour ago <before an hour> and [then] went [out].
ma qāl-lī-š 'iši.	He didn't say anything to me.

– biddi arūḥ…	– I want to go …
– il-māma ma btismaḥ,	– Mum <the mum> won't let [you]!
il-māma btismaḥ-lek?	Does [your] mum let you <allow to-you>?
– yā māma, 'ismaḥī-li[6] arūḥ…	– Mum, let me go…
– ṭayyeb, basmaḥ-lek, bass	– OK, I'll let you, but take care on the way
dīri bālek fi-ṭ-ṭarīq.	<pay your-attention in the way>.
– 'ismaḥ-li[6] aqul-lak…	– Do you mind my telling you … <allow me that I tell you…>
– 'ismaḥ-li bil-jarīde!	– Could I have the newspaper <allow me in the newspaper>?

----

matal[7] *(proverb)*:

'illi b^{y}izra^{c} hawa, b^{y}uḥṣod zawābe^{c}. *He who sows the wind will reap storms.*

---

6. See **Explanations 3**, below.
7. Compare with Hosea chapter VIII, verse 7 in the Bible:
"For they have sown the wind and they shall reap the whirlwind."

Explanations

1. On days and months

The plural of **yōm** is **'ayyām** or **-iyyām**, but after the numbers 3-10 a helping **-t** is added:

five days	ḫam^{e}s + t + -iyyām	= ḫam^{e}st‿iyyām
seven days	sabe^c + t + -iyyām	= sabe^{c}t‿iyyām
three days	talat + t + -iyyām	= talatt‿iyyām (or tlatt-iyyām)

The same thing happens to **'ašhor** or **-ušhor**, the plural form of the word **šaher**, which means *month*. It, too, takes on a special form after the numbers 3-10: ḫam^{e}s + t + -ušhor = ḫam^{e}st‿ušhor (ḫamst‿ušhor).

'arba^{c}t‿ušhor,	tamant‿ušhor,	tis^a^{c}t‿ušhor (= ti-sa^c-tuš-hor)
four months	*eight months*	*nine months*

Now for a trick question. How do you say *24 months*? You'll find the answer at the end of the lesson.

2. On taxes...

It's interesting to note that the word *tax* – **ḍarībe** – is derived from the root **ḍ-r-b** (*hit, beat*). We've got to pay tax to the authorities and that's definitely a blow! But the usual word for *blow* is **ḍarbe**.

3. law samaḥt

The literal meaning of **law samaḥt** is *if you permitted, if you would allow*. This is a very common expression used to beg pardon for bothering someone, or request permission to ask or do something: *if possible, ... if you would permit me ...* When said loudly in a tone of rebuke, **law samaḥt!** is the equivalent of the English *Would you mind?!* with the implication *Please be quiet!*

By the way, **samaḥ** [**yismaḥ**] is another example of a verb whose second vowel is *a* in the present-future tense. If you look back at Lesson 12, you will notice that all these verbs have a **guttural sound** or an **emphatic consonant** such as ^{c} , ' , ḥ, as the second or third root letter. These sounds "like" the vowel *a*; just think of the verbs **yib^{c}at, yiftaḥ, yis'al**.

We'll discuss the imperative **'ismaḥ** in Lesson 17 (Book 2).

4. More on the helping vowel – this time before bti-, bni- (mni-)...

You'll recall the helping vowel ^{e} which is inserted between consonants to avoid "tongue twisters," in other words, clusters of consonants with no vowels between them. You'll remember the example: **bi**nt + kb**ī**re → **bi**nt‿^{e}kb**ī**re. It's virtually impossible to say bi|ntkb|**ī**re. Likewise, though it's not so hard to say l**ē**š fat**a**ḥt? (*Why did you open?*), it is hard to say l**ē**š bt**i**ftaḥ? (*Why are you opening?*). The solution is to say l**ē**š‿^{e}bt**i**ftaḥ?

Let's compare the following sentences:

Every day I do laundry	k**u**ll y**ō**m b**a**ġsel
Every day she does laundry	k**u**ll y**ō**m‿^{e}bt**i**ġsel
Afterwards I open	ba^{c}d**ē**n b**a**ftaḥ
Afterwards she kneads (dough to make bread)	ba^{c}d**ē**n‿^{e}bt**i**^{c}jen

Exercises

A. Pronunciation exercise

Add the helping vowel ^{e} (if needed, i.e., where there are three consonants together without an intervening vowel). Translate the result into English and check your answers against the key to the exercises.

1. l**ē**š b**i**ddak tr**ū**ḥ?
2. bitš**ū**f mn**ī**ḥ min h**ō**n?
3. kull y**ō**m bt**i**kteb d**a**rsak?
4. n**a**^{c}am, kull y**ō**m b**a**kteb d**a**rsi.
5. '**ē**š bt**u**ṭlob minno?
6. b**a**ṭlob kt**ā**b jd**ī**d.

If you got the last one right, well done! It shows you have caught on and are becoming sensitive to the rhythmic flow of the sentence. If you didn't succeed, never mind – after a few more lessons and exercises, it will sink in.

B. Translate into English:

7. l**ā**zem t**i**dfa^{c} kull š**a**h^{e}r.
8. muš l**ā**zem t**i**dfa^{c} h**a**llaq, m**u**mken t**i**dfa^{c} mɑrrɑ t**ā**nye.
9. il-b**i**sse (the cat) hɑrbɑt min il-b**ē**t, šu bitq**ū**l?
10. ṭɑyyeb rɑbɑṭna‿l-k**a**lb, muš m**u**mken n**u**rboṭ il-b**i**sse kam**ā**n.

C. Translate into Arabic:

11. Has he paid? No, he hasn't paid / he hasn't paid yet.
12. He always pays, but today he doesn't want to pay.
13. If he pays – fine. If he doesn't pay, we'll write to his mother.
14. Samira's asking the time <asking how-much [is] the hour>.
15. She asks me for money. – And she's asked me for money, too <and from me, too, she asked-for money>.
16. Boy, why are you hitting children <the children> in the street?
17. Me <I>? I'm not hitting anybody (ḥ**a**da).

Let's not forget the promised exercises on the word illi. Use the following model:

j**i**bt‿il-ḥal**ī**b – il-ḥal**ī**b illi j**i**bto
š**u**fna‿l-b**ē**t – il-b**ē**t illi šufn**ā**^{h}

For now we'll make do with just a few sentences:

18. zar**a**^{c}na duħħ**ā**n – id-duħħ**ā**n illi za-…
19. daf**a**^{c}tu ḍɑr**ī**be – iḍ-ḍɑr**ī**be illi da-…
20. Y**ū**sef, daf**a**^{c}et l-^{e}ḥs**ā**b? – l-^{e}ḥs**ā**b illi da-…
21. M**a**ryam, daf**a**^{c}ti l-^{e}ḥs**ā**b? – l-^{e}ḥs**ā**b illi da-…

Note: In the flow of speech, the i- of illi is usually unstressed, and sometimes even drops after a vowel. We say:

iḍ-ḍɑr**ī**be illi dafa^{c}n**ā**-ha or iḍ-ḍɑr**ī**be‿lli dafa^{c}n**ā**-ha

----

So far we've studied 13 lessons. Let's say that in Arabic:

la-ḥ**a**dd il-y**ō**m, dar**a**sna … (?)

We're familiar with the numbers 'iḥd**ɑ**^{ce}š, tn**ɑ**^{ce}š (also pronounced ṭn**ɑ**^{ce}š) and talatt**ɑ**^{ce}š, in which the ending ^{ce}š is a short form of ^{c}**ɑ**šɑr. When a noun comes after the numbers 11-19, the word appears in full –'iḥd**ɑ**^{c}š<u>ɑr</u>, tn**ɑ**^{c}šɑr… tisa^{c}t**ɑ**^{c}šɑr.

Don't forget that after the numbers 11-100 (see page 59) the noun is singular, so *13 lessons* is talatt**ɑ**^{c}šɑr d**a**rs, and *15 days* is ħam^{e}st**ɑ**^{c}šɑr y**ō**m.

And the answer to the question: How do you say *24 months*?
'**a**rb^{c}a u-^{c}išr**ī**n š**a**h^{e}r, of course!

id-dars ir-rābeˁ ˁašɑr – dars 'arbɑˁtɑˁeš

The Fourteenth Lesson (Lesson Fourteen)

Have you been wondering why the stress falls on the **first** syllable of ka-ta-b and ka-ta-bu, but on the **second** syllable of kat**a**bt and kat**a**bna? Close inspection will reveal that in both ka-**tab**-t and ka-**tab**-na the final -b of the root is followed not by a vowel, but by **another consonant** (-bt- and -bn-). Imagine this pair of consonants as a hurdle that you have to jump in order to pronounce the word. The syllable before it acts like a springboard that bounces you over, and in consequence it receives the stress.

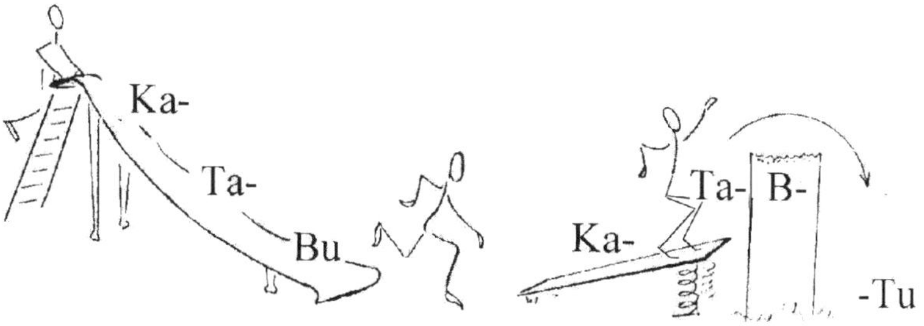

The cartoon is meant to help you visualize the explanation, but if it doesn't appeal to you, just ignore it!

Let's restate the rule:
  When two consonants occur together with no intervening vowel,
  the stress falls on the syllable that precedes them.

Compare, for example:
  t**a**-ra-ku   *they left*
  ta-r**a**<u>kn</u>a   *we left*

In tar**a**kna, the syllable -rak- has acquired the stress. The same situation arises when, for example, we add most of the attached pronouns to the verb:
  t**a**rak + -ni → tar**a**k-ni   *he left me*

Note that this doesn't happen with the attached pronouns -ak, -ek and -o because they start with a vowel:
  t**a**-ra-kak – t**a**-ra-kek – t**a**-ra-ko   *he left you*ᵐ */ you*ᶠ */ him*

This rule will help you to understand the changes that take place in the following sentences:

■   tarak 'ibno? – '**ā**, ta-ra-ko   *Did he leave his son? – Yes, he left him.*

t**a**rak mɑrɑto? –'**a**ywa, ta-r**a**k-ha	*Did he leave his wife? – Yes, he left her.*
t**a**rak 'awl**ā**do?	*Did he leave his children?*
– n**a**^{c}am, tar**a**k-hom	*– Yes, he left them.*
t**a**rkat il-b**i**nt? – '**ɑ̄**, tark**a**t-ha.	*Did she leave the girl? – Yes, she left her.*
l**ā**zem t**u**rboṭ iš-š**a**nta.	*You need to tie up the suitcase.*
l**ā**zem turb**o**ṭ-ha.	*You need to tie it up.*

The same thing happens when we add -li, -lak, -lek, -lo etc. to a verb, in effect creating a single word:

k**a**tab + li → kat**a**b-li	*He wrote to me*
k**a**tbat + lo → katb**a**t-lo	*She wrote to him*
b^{y}**u**ktob + lak → b^{y}ukt**o**b-lak	*He writes to you*

This rule applies to all words – not just to verbs. For example:

b**a**lad	*settlement, town, village*
b**a**-la-di, b**a**-la-do	*my town, his village*
ba-l**a**d-kom	*your town / village*

Please be reassured, as always, that you don't need to make an effort to memorize this rule. It's enough to note the phenomenon and understand to some extent what's happening. You'll internalize the rule through listening to the recording and repeating the conversations and examples out loud, as well as by completing the exercises, lesson by lesson.

Vocabulary

qann**ī**ne [qan**ā**ni]	bottle	su'**ā**l ['**a**s'ile]	question
d**a**faš [y**i**dfeš]	to push	dukk**ā**n(e) [dakāk**ī**n]	shop
kazz**ā**b [kazzāb**ī**n]	liar	š**a**nta [šant**ā**t] or [šan**ā**ti]	suitcase; bag

Conversation

– m**ī**n k**a**sar il-qann**ī**ne illi[1] k**ā**nat ^{c}a-ṭ-t**ɑ̄**wle?	– Who broke the bottle that was on the table?
– Y**ū**sef kas**a**r-ha!	– Yusef broke it[f].

---

1. See **Explanations 2** below.

– kazzābe[2]! 'ana kasart-ha?!	– Liar! **I** broke it?!
baba! Maryam kasrat	Dad! Maryam broke
il-qannīne u-hallaq bitqūl	the bottle and now she's saying
inno 'ana‿lli kasart-ha.	I broke it <that I [am] who broke it>.
hiyye‿lli kasrat-ha,	She's the one who broke it!
btikser kull 'iši fi-l-bēt!	She breaks everything in the house!
– bass! biddi as'al Maryam,	– Enough! I want to ask Maryam,
biddi as'al-ha.	I want to ask her.
ya Maryam, biddi as'alek su'āl.	Maryam, I want to ask you a question.
'inti‿lli kasarti‿l-qannīne	Was it you who broke the bottle,
willa mīn?	or [if not] who [did]?
'iza kasartī-ha, qulī-li.	If you broke it, tell me.
– ya^{c}ni Yūsef dafaš-ni u-…	– Er… Yusef pushed me and …
– hēk?	– That's how it was <thus>?
dafašek?	He pushed you?
il-ḥaqq ^{c}alēh?	He's to blame <the right is against him>?
ma^{c}alešš… ya Yūsef,	Never mind… Yusef, [it's] not nice
muš‿^{e}mnīḥ tidfeš 'uḫtak!	to push <that you push> your sister!
– bass hiyye dafšat-ni, hiyye…	– But she pushed me, she …
– bass! rūḥ jīb qannīne	– That's enough! Go [and] get a bottle from
min id-dukkān u-ḫalaṣ!	the shop and we'll say no more about it <it's finished>!

The incident is over. Let's pick up … not the broken bottle, but a few interesting details, paying particular attention to changes in stress!

Explanations

1. Notes on some words

kazzāb [kazzābīn]	*liar*
kazab [yikzeb] ^{c}ala…	*to lie to*

2. The masculine form is kazzāb. *That [man] is a liar!* is hāda kazzāb! In literary Arabic and in rural areas, however, it is pronounced hāḏa kaḏḏāb!, i.e., with ḏ in both cases (see **Abbreviations,** p.[10]). This shows that in urban speech ḏ turns into d in some words (e.g. hāda) and into z in others (e.g. kazzāb).

kazab ^{c}al**a**yy	*He lied to me*
b^{y}**i**kzeb ^{c}al**ē**ki	*He's lying to you*
k**i**z^{e}b [kizb**ā**t]	*lie, falsehood*
kull h**ā**da k**i**z^{e}b	*That's all lies* <all that's a lie>!
ђαlαṣ [yuђloṣ]	*to finish / come to an end*
ђαlαṣ!	*It's over! That's it! Enough!*
'iza 'inte bitq**ū**l, ђαlαṣ!	*If **you** say [so], it's enough! (There's no more to be said, I believe it.)*
'**a**yya s**ē**^{c}a btu**ђ**loṣ iṣ-ṣ**α**lα[3]?	*What time do prayers* <does the prayer> *finish?*
^{e}mb**ā**reḥ ђ**α**lṣαt[4] bakk**ī**r	*Yesterday they* <it> *finished early.*

2. illi again

Do you remember the m**a**tal in the previous lesson? When illi is the first word in a sentence, the initial i- is stressed ('**i**lli) and it means *He who..., Whoever...* Here's another example:

■ '**i**lli q**a**l-lak h**ē**k, kazz**ā**b — *Whoever told you that* <thus> *[is] a liar*

But when illi follows a noun, it is not stressed (illi) and after a vowel the first i generally drops:

il-w**a**lad illi k**a**sαr h**ā**da... — *The boy who broke that ...*
iṣ-ṣ**α**bi‿lli k**a**sαr h**ā**da…

3. Stress

Note the changes in stress that occur throughout the lesson:

■ k**a**sar → kas**a**r-ha
k**a**srat → kasr**a**t-ha
k**a**sar → kas**a**rti → kasart**ī**-ha

Likewise, b^{y}**i**s'al / b**i**s'al → bis'**a**l-ni → ma bis'al-n**ī**-š

And similarly: tar**a**k-na (*he left us*). And now you can see that the word tar**a**kna has two meanings:

---

3. The word ṣ**α**lα (ṣal**ā**^{h} in literary Arabic) means *prayer*, plural [ṣαlαw**α**t].
4. This is the pronunciation in the Jerusalem area. And in Galilee? We'll find out soon.

tar**a**kna *We left*

tar**a**k-na *He left us*

The context will show you which sense is intended:

■ tar**a**kna u-r**ā**ḥ *He left us and went [away].*

tar**a**kna‿l-w**a**lad fi-l-b**ē**t *We left the boy at home.*

Completion exercise

– d**a**han [y**i**dhan] *to paint* (with oil or plastic paint)*; to coat*

1. d**a**hanu‿l-b**ē**t? – '**ā**, d-... *Did they paint the house? – Yes, they painted it.*
2. d**a**hanu‿d-d**ā**r[5]? – '**a**ywa d-... *Did they paint the house? – Yes, they painted it.*
3. b**i**ddo y**i**dhan il-b**ā**b *He wants to paint the door,*
4. w-iš-šubb**ā**k kam**ā**n b**i**ddo yi-... *and he wants to paint the window, too*
5. b**a**dhan iṭ-ṭ**ā**wle, ba-... *I'll paint the table, I'll paint it.*
   l**a**', ma[6] tid-... *No! Don't paint it!*

[See lesson 13]

– m**a**za^c [y**i**mza^c] *to tear*

6. m**a**za^c l-^{e}kt**ā**b? l**ē**š m-...? *Did he tear the book? Why did he tear it?*
7. ma maz**a**^{c}eš l-^{e}kt**ā**b, *He didn't tear the book,*
   ma ma....-š. *he didn't tear it.*
8. w-il-jar**ī**de, m**ī**n m-... ha? *And the newspaper, who tore it^f?*
9. ma t-... -š! *Don't tear it^f!*

---

5. Remember, d**ā**r is feminine.

6. Don't...! The negative imperative can be expressed by means of ma... -š (or simply m**a**...) with the verb in the subjunctive (implying intention, desire, prohibition, etc.). For example, *Don't write!* is ma t**i**kteb-š! (m**a** t**i**kteb!$^{\#}$)

– With illi (*that, which* – relative pronoun) / inno (*that* – conjunction):

10. qal-li ….. dahan iṭ-ṭɑ̄wle.	*He told me that he painted the table.*
11. wēn iṭ-ṭɑ̄wle ….. dahan-ha?	*Where's the table that he painted?*
12. il-ulād mazaᶜu ktāb.	*The children tore a book.*
13. hayy l-ektāb … mazaᶜū^h	*Here's the book that they tore <it>.*

Note:

Have you been unsure about adding the two different forms of the attached pronoun *him / it* to a verb? Remember: the rule is -o after a consonant and -h after -a, -i, or -u. The following table should help you keep things straight in your mind:

tarak + -o → tarako	*He left him*
taraku + -h → tarakū^h	*They left him*
tarakt + -o → tarakto	*You^m left him*
tarakti + -h → taraktī^h	*You^f left him*
tarakna + -h → taraknā^h	*We left him*

Here are a few more sentences for you to complete:

– rɑkɑḍ [yurkoḍ]	*to run*
14. 'ana rɑkɑḍet bass huwwe ma rɑkɑḍ or ma ra- …š.	*I ran but he didn't run.*
15. u-hiyye kamān rɑkḍɑt? – la', ma ra-…	*And did she run, too?* *– No, she didn't run.*
16. lāzem yurkoḍ, bass 'inte, ma t-…	*He has to run but don't you run* *<but you, don't run>!*

– **ja**ma^{c} [y**i**jma^{c}]	*to collect / gather*
17. bt**i**jma^{c} ṭɑw**ɑ̄**be^{c} [8]?	*Do you collect stamps?*
jibt**i**-llak ṭ**ɑ̄**be^{c} ḥ**i**lu.	*I've brought you a beautiful stamp!*
18. 'aђ**ū**y kam**ā**n b-…ṭɑw**ɑ̄**be^{c}	*My brother collects stamps, too.*
19. b^{y}ij- … fi d**a**ftɑr	*He collects them in an exercise book.*
20. kull l-ewl**ā**d b^{y}**i**jma^{c}u ṭɑw**ɑ̄**be^{c}?	*Do all the children collect stamps?*
21. l**a**', ul**ā**d il-jir**ɑ̄**n, m**a**t̠alan[9]	*No, the neighbors' children, for example,*
ma b^{y}ij- …š ṭɑw**ɑ̄**be^{c}.	*don't collect stamps.*

These exercises may seem rather boring, but they are essential. They teach you to express yourself freely and help you to find your way quickly and easily around the various grammatical forms. This book does not set out to teach you rigid sentences and expressions that you have to learn by heart. After all, you don't want to be like the immigrant newly arrived in England who memorized such complicated sentences as: *She sells sea shells by the sea shore*, and *Peter Piper picked a peck of pickled peppers.* Reciting them to a friend, he confided: "But it's hard to work them into a conversation!"

Pianists play scales and singers do voice exercises. Your exercises are just as demanding – but they disturb the neighbors less!

---

8. ṭ**ɑ̄**be^{c} [ṭɑw**ɑ̄**be^{c}] means *stamp*, from the root ṭ-b-^{c} (*to print*).
m**ɑ**ṭbɑ^{c}ɑ means *printing house.*

9. In literary Arabic, m**a**t̠alan. In urban speech, the sound t̠ turns into t or s depending on the word, the locality, and – the speaker! Sometimes two words derived from the same root even have s in one word and t in another. On page 71 we learned the word ḥ**ā**des, *accident* (literary Arabic, ḥ**ā**det̠) and on page 87 m**a**tal, *proverb*.
The expression *for example* can be pronounced m**a**t̠alan, m**a**talan or m**a**salan.

id-dars il-ḫ**ā**mes ᶜ**α**šαr – dars ḫamestαᶜeš

15

The Fifteenth Lesson (Lesson Fifteen)

Let's take a break from verbs and take a look at the **comparative** form of the adjective, i.e., *more… than.* We already know that *nicer than…* is '**a**ḥla min (**Lesson 10, Explanations 2**).

Adjectives usually adopt a special form to express the comparative. The pattern is '**a**□□a□, '**a**□□α□, or '**α**□□α□, depending on how the consonants in the word affect the vowels[1]. The word kt**ī**r (*much, many*) changes to '**a**ktαr *(more)*. In the case of ḥ**i**lu, the final -u changes to -a, and the same thing happens to all adjectives ending in -u, or -i; in other words, the comparative form of adjectives like these is '**a**□□a.

However, not all Arabic adjectives change their form in the comparative; some add '**a**ktαr (*more*) after the adjective instead, just as in English we say *bigger* and *taller* but *more distant, more desirable*:

mašġ**ū**l	mašġ**ū**l '**a**ktαr
busy	*busier* <more busy>

Vocabulary

kb**ī**r (cp '**a**kbαr)[2]	big; old	ṣ**α**bi [ṣeby**ā**n][4]	boy, youth
ṭαw**ī**l (cp '**α**ṭwαl)	long; tall	f**ō**q	above
zġ**ī**r (cp '**a**zġαr)	small; young	ᶜ**ē**le / ᶜ**ā**'ile	family
qαṣ**ī**r (cp '**α**qṣαr)[3]	short	[ᶜā'il**ā**t/ ᶜiy**ā**l]	families
enḍ**ī**f (cp '**α**nḍαf)	clean	ᶜ**u**mor / ᶜ**u**mer	age; life
qar**ī**b (cp '**α**qrαb)[3]	near	ᶜ**u**mri[5]	my age; my life
f**i**ker	thought; opinion	mitj**a**wwez	married[m]
tam**ā**m	precisely, exactly	mitj**a**w(w)ze	married[f]
ma ᶜ**a**da	except, apart from, aside from		

1. Take a look at the end of Lesson 8, and join the "curious."

2. The comparative will be indicated by the abbreviation "cp".

3. You will often hear people say h**α**qṣαr instead of '**α**qṣαr, and this is the case with every adjective whose first root letter is q. People do this so as to avoid having to pronounce two glottal stops ('**α**'ṣαr) immediately after each other (remember, q- is pronounced like '- by urban speakers).

4. The vowel sound *e* is so strongly affected by the ṣ that you will hear it almost as ṣo-.

Conversation

– kam[6] walad ᶜindak, ya ’abu Fahīm?	– How many children have you got, Abu Fahim?
– ᶜindi ђams‿ewlād[7], talt‿ewlād u-bintēn.	– I’ve got five children: three sons and two daughters.
– mīn ’akbɑr wāḥad?	– Who’s the oldest <biggest one>?
– Fahīm ’akbɑr wāḥad, bass huwwe qɑṣīr, hɑqṣɑr min il-walad it-tāni.	– Fahim’s the oldest <one>, but he’s short, shorter than the second boy.
– w-it-tāni, šū ’ismo?	– What’s the second boy’s name <and the second, what his-name>?
– ’ismo Nabīl, huwwe ’azġɑr min Fahīm, bass ’ɑṭwɑl minno.[8]	– His name’s Nabil, he’s younger <smaller> than Fahim, but taller than him.

---

5. ᶜumᵒr / ᶜumᵉr + attached pronoun + the negative particle ma = *never [in my life]*. For example: ᶜumri ma šufteš sabeᶜ – *I’ve never* <in my life I haven’t> *seen a lion.*
ᶜumro ma šaf-š … – *He’s never seen …. / He’d never seen…*
ᶜumᵉr-ha ma šāfat-š…– *She’s never seen… She’d never seen…*

6. kam or ’akam means *how much / how many*, and the noun being asked about is always singular. See **Explanations 1.**

7. walad means *boy*, but its plural ewlād / ulād can mean either *children (girls and boys)* or just *boys*. Notice that Abu Fahim uses ulād the first time to mean *children* and the second time to mean *sons*. The phrase ma ᶜindō-š ulād is ambiguous; if it is intended to mean *He has no sons*, you could add ᶜindo bass banāt *He’s only got daughters.*

8. You can confirm this by looking at the drawing.

– qaddēš ᶜ**u**mro, l-ᵉkb**ī**r?	– What age is the older [boy] <how much his-age the big [one] >?
– Fah**ī**m, ᶜ**u**mro s**a**bᶜa u-ᶜišr**ī**n	– Fahim’s 27 <Fahim his-age 27 year>
s**a**ne u-Nab**ī**l, tal**ā**te u-ᶜišr**ī**n,	and Nabil’s 23,
y**a**ᶜni, ’**a**zġɑr min ’aђ**ū**ʰ	that’s to say, four years younger
ᵉb-’**ar**bɑᶜ‿ᵉsn**ī**n.[9]	than his brother.
– u-baᶜd**ē**n?	– And after that?
– baᶜd**ē**n il-ban**ā**t:	– Then [there are] the girls:
K**ā**mle u-Wid**ā**d	Kāmla *(perfect)* and Widād *(affection)*
u-**ā**ђer w**ā**ḥad iṣ-ṣ**ɑ**bi, Ḥ**a**nna,	And the last one, the boy, Hanna,
b**a**ᶜdo // liss**ā**to zġ**ī**r	he’s still young
ᶜ**u**mro ᶜ**a**šr‿ᵉsn**ī**n.	[only] ten years old.
– m**a** š**ā**’ (ɑ)ll**ɑ̄**h,[10] ᶜ**ē**le kb**ī**re.	– Touch wood, a big family.
’**ɑ**llɑ iђall**ī**-lak ewl**ā**dak! [11]	May God preserve your children for you!
– ’**ɑ**llɑ y**i**ḥfɑẓek!	– Thank you <May God preserve you>.

– qaddēš ᶜ**u**mrak ’**i**nte?	– How old are you <How much your-age, you>?
– š**ū** f**i**krak?	– What do you think <what your-thought>?
’**a**na ’**a**kbɑr m**i**nnak?	Am I older than you?
– l**a**’, ’**a**na ’**a**kbɑr m**i**nnak‿ᵉb-s**a**ne,	– No, I’m a year older than you,
w**i**lla ’**a**na ġɑlṭ**ɑ̄**n?	if I’m not mistaken <or [am] I wrong>?
– mɑẓb**ū**ṭ, ’**a**na ’**a**zġɑr m**i**nnak	– Right, I’m younger <smaller> than you,
bass il-f**a**rᵉq b**ē**n-na m**u**š s**a**ne.	but the difference between us isn’t a year.
’**a**na baq**ū**l: t**a**mant‿**u**šhor.[12]	I would say eight months.

---

9. Pronounced eb-’**ar**-ba-ᶜes-n**ī**n. Try saying this slowly, and don’t forget to put the stress on the two syllables ’**ar** and n**ī**n

10. Literally, *what God wanted* (in literary Arabic). This is an expression of admiration, with the implication of averting the evil eye. It means: *This is God’s will, and I’m not envious. I don’t want to bring you bad luck.*

11. iђ**a**lli: we’ll explain this verbal form later. This expression is often used when speaking to people about their children. To a woman, of course, you would say ’**ɑ**llɑ iђall**ī**-lek ewl**ā**dek!

12. See **Lesson 13, Explanations 1**.

– mu**š** muh**e**mm.	– [It's] not important.

– w**ē**n sākn**ī**n ewl**ā**dak?	– Where do your children live?
– kullay**ā**t-hen // k**u**ll-hom sākn**ī**n	– They all live with me
m**a**ᶜi fi-l-b**ē**t had**ā**k[13] l-ᵉkb**ī**r	in that big house next to the
j**a**mb il-m**a**drase, ma ᶜ**a**da	school, except [for]
K**ā**mle. h**i**yye mitj**a**wwze	Kāmla. She's married
u-s**ā**kne maᶜ j**ō**z-ha fi b**ē**t	and lives with her husband in a smaller
'**a**zġɑr bass‿ejd**ī**d w-ᵉnḍ**ī**f u-ḥ**i**lu.	house, but [it's] new and clean and nice.
– ᵉbᶜ**ī**d ᶜan[14] b**ē**t-kom?	– [Is it] far from your house?
– l**a**', qar**ī**b‿ᵉkt**ī**r min[15] b**ē**tna.	– No, very near our house.
y**a**mm[16] ḥadd**ī**-na (j**a**mb-na).	Right next to us.
il-bēt**ē**n jamb b**ɑ**ᶜᵉḍ tam**ā**m.	The two houses are literally <exactly> next door to each other <one beside the other>
– u-b**ē**t 'aḫ**ū**k?	– And your brother's house?
– b**ē**to '**a**bᶜad‿ᵉšw**a**yy	– His house is a little farther [away],
f**ō**q ᶜa-l-j**a**bal.	up on the hill.

Explanations

1. How much, how many

Let's start by looking at the difference between kam and qadd**ē**š:

– qadd**ē**š is used to ask about quantity (*how much?*);

– kam is used to ask about the number of individual units (*how many?*).

---

13. *That (big house)* – an explanation will be given in the next lesson. Let's just say for the moment that although had**ā**k means *that*, h**ā**da and h**ā**di, too, often translate best into English as *that.*

14. We've already met the preposition ᶜan, on page 41. It means *from*, in contexts involving distancing or separation, while the preposition min relates to a thing's origin or starting point.

15. Note that while in English we say *near to*, in Arabic we say qar**ī**b min <near from>. *Near here* is qar**ī**b min h**ō**n.

16. yamm = *right, exactly*. yamm f**ō**q! = *right at the top!* yamm h**ē**k! = *exactly so* (*and not otherwise*)! The word b**ɑ**ᶜᵉḍ (*one another*) will be explained in Book 2.

kam is followed by a singular noun (*how many boy, how many book*?), or by the word wāḥad (*one*) when the question relates to something that has already been mentioned (– *I saw[some] books. – How many* <one>*?)*. Instead of kam you will sometimes hear people say ’akam / ’akam.

biddi rozz	*I want [some] rice*
qaddēš biddak?	*How much do you want?*
ya^{c}ni kam kīlo?	*I mean, how many kilo[s]?*
kam bēḍɑ biddak?	*How many eggs do you want?*

Similarly, kam yōm / kam sane / kam mɑrrɑ = *how many days / how many years / how many times?*

kam / ’akam min… can also mean *a few*:

ba^{ce}d kam yōm	*a few days later* <after a few days> / *in a few days*
’akam min bēḍɑ	*a few eggs*

2. Bigger, the biggest (the comparative and the superlative adjective)

At the beginning of the lesson we saw how the comparative is formed. Note that this is an invariable form that remains unchanged regardless of whether it refers to a masculine, feminine or plural noun:

■ walad ’akbɑr — bint ’akbɑr — ulād ’akbɑr
a bigger boy — *a bigger girl* — *bigger children*

Now let’s learn how to translate *the biggest boy*. You can say (as in literary Arabic) il-walad il-’akbɑr, but in colloquial Arabic it’s more usual to say ’akbɑr walad, i.e., to drop the definite article and put the comparative adjective before the noun.

■ biddi bēt ’akbɑr	*I want a bigger house*
hāda ’akbɑr bēt	*That’s the biggest house*
walad šɑ̄ṭer[17]	*a clever boy*
hū ’ašṭɑr minnak	*He’s smarter than you*
huwwe ’ašṭɑr walad fi-ṣ-ṣɑff	*He’s the smartest boy in the class*
jībi ktāb ’akbɑr!	*Bring a bigger book!*
hāda ’akbɑr wāḥad	*This is the biggest one*

---

17. šɑ̄ṭer (cp ’ašṭɑr), fem šɑ̄ṭrɑ, pl [šɑ̄ṭrīn] means *clever, smart; hard working; talented; quick*. You call a boy šɑ̄ṭer to encourage him, or to praise him for something done well. It is also used as a form of address to a boy: – jib-li… ya šɑ̄ṭer! (*Clever boy! Please bring me ...*).

This construction will remind you of what we said about **tā**ni w**a**lad, *the second boy* – see **Lesson 10, Explanations 1**. In the final sentence above, the word w**ā**ḥad (or w**ā**ḥed), *one*, is used, just as in English, instead of repeating the word previously mentioned.

Another example: You want to buy notebooks. After choosing the kind you want, you tell the shopkeeper:

b**i**ddi talat**ī**n w**ā**ḥad — *I want 30* (of them) <30 ones>

And you don't mean 31, of course! In Arabic, *thirty-one* is w**ā**ḥad u-talat**ī**n.

3. Big / old

The adjective kb**ī**r has more than one sense: it means *big* (mad**ī**ne kb**ī**re is *a big city*), and *important* (*a big man*), as well as *old / adult*, so sometimes we need to add an explanatory phrase to make the meaning clear:

■ h**u**wwe '**a**kbɑr m**i**nni fi-l-^{c}**u**m^{o}r — *He is older than me* <bigger than me in age>.

4. Between

The Arabic word beyn is used in the same way as *between* in English:

■ b**ē**ni u-b**ē**nak	*between you and me* <me and you> / *between ourselves (I can tell you...)*
il-mas**ā**fe b**ē**n it-t^{e}n**ē**n	*the distance between the two*
b**ē**n il-b**ā**b w-iš-šubb**ā**k	*between the door and the window*

When a plural pronoun (-na, -kom, etc.) is attached to it, **bēn** can assume either one of two alternative forms: **bēn** or **bēnāt-**.

■ il-f**a**r^{e}q b**ē**n-na / bēn**ā**t-na — *the difference between us*
b**ē**n-kom / bēn**ā**t-kom — *between you* ^{pl}

5. All of us, all of you…

k**u**ll-na	*all of us*
k**u**ll-ku // k**u**ll-kom	*all of you*
k**u**ll-hen // k**u**ll-hom	*all of them*

In the Galilee region you will often hear people saying kullay**ā**t-na, kullay**ā**t-ku, kullay**ā**t-hen

Exercises

A. Translate into English:

1. b**ē**to '**ɑ**nḍɑf min b**ē**tak.
2. h**ā**da '**ɑ**nḍɑf b**ē**t fi-l-b**a**lad.
3. h**ā**di '**a**kbɑr b**ē**ḍɑ.
4. h**ā**da l**ō**n '**a**ḥla, b^{y}i^{c}jeb-ni '**a**ktɑr.
5. b**i**nti mitj**a**w(w)ze.
6. m**ī**n j**ō**z b**i**ntak, u k**ī**f h**u**wwe?
7. m**a** f**ī**^{h} f**a**r^{e}q b**ē**n it-t^{e}n**ē**n.
8. '**i**nte ġɑlṭ**ɑ̄**n. – l**a**', '**i**nti‿l-ġɑlṭ**ɑ̄**ne <you [are] the mistaken-one^{f}>!
9. k**u**llna š**u**fna‿l-f**i**l^{e}m, ma ^{c}**a**da Y**ū**sef.
10. ^{c}**u**mro ma d**a**fa^{c} ḍɑr**ɑ̄**yeb. (See Lesson 12, p.79).

B. Complete the sentences

(Replace the English words with the appropriate expression in Arabic):

11. (Never) ma r**u**ḥt-^{e}š ^{c}a-s-s**ī**nama.
12. (How many times) š**u**f^{e}t hal-f**i**l^{e}m?
13. (How much) b**i**ddak t**i**dfa^{c}?
14. f**ī**^{h} b**i**nt '**a**kbɑr (than you^{f})?
15. m**ī**n (is the biggest / oldest)?
16. h**u**wwe '**a**kbɑr m**i**nni b-(two months).
17. f**ī**^{h} ^{c}**i**ndo ṭɑw**ɑ̄**be^{c} (more) m**i**nni.

18. il-yōm id-dars ([is] longer).
19. la’, muš ’ɑṭwɑl, (the same <thing>)
20. (Yes!), hāda dars (very long).

C. Translate into Arabic:

21. How old are you^{m} <how much [is] your age>?
22. How old is your^{m} son <your son – how-much his-age>?
23. How many years were you^{m} with him <how many years you were at him [at his house]>?
24. How many <how-many one> have you^{pl} got?
25. Who’s the elder, you^{m} or him?
26. He’s older than me, but I’m taller than him.
27. How many times were you^{m} there?
28. I’ve never seen a cleverer boy <a boy cleverer – never I saw>!
29. How many families are there in the village?
30. No more than seventy.
31. Who was last <last one^{m} >?
32. There’s no difference between the two.
33. Did you^{m} open the shop yesterday?
34. I want a nicer one^{m}.
35. I want the nicest one^{m}.
36. He has bigger books.
37. That’s the biggest book.
38. What’s the difference between the two books?
39. They say there’s a big difference.

Revision Exercise on the Subjunctive

Have a look back at Lesson 5, Explanations 1 and Exercise B, and Lesson 6, Explanations 2.

Now let's take some of the verbs we learned in Lessons 5-15 and put them into the correct form after the following expressions:

*	ḥ**a**tta…	*so that …*
**	m**ī**n q**a**l-lak inno…	*Who told you that…*
*	muš l**ā**zem…	*It's not necessary that ….*
**	biq**ū**l inno…	*He says that …*

1. … so that you'll^{m} see your brother.
2. Who told you^{m} that you would see your brother tomorrow?
3. He mustn't see you^{f}!
4. He says he'll see you^{f} tomorrow.
5. … so that they visit the museum.
6. Who told you^{m} they're visiting my uncle?
7. He doesn't need to send the letter now.
8. He says he'll send it^{m} later.
9. He doesn't need to pay the whole sum.
10. He says he'll pay tomorrow.
11. Who told you^{m} he pays every month?
12. … so that you^{m} pay the same amount.
13. Who told you^{m} they would be at home?
14. … so that they'll be happy.
15. It's not necessary for them to be <that they be> at the same school.
16. He says they'll be with you^{m} <at you> tomorrow.

*	Intention or prohibition:	subjunctive (without b- prefix)
**	Statement of fact:	present-future (with b- prefix)

"Snowball" Exercise

A good way to learn to express yourself is to begin with a short phrase and, once you feel comfortable with it, start adding a few words before and after it to make a longer sentence, just like a snowball picking up more snow as it rolls along. For instance, if you want to say with confidence: *My dad says you've got to go and bring a chair for your mum*, you can build the sentence up in the steps below (repeating each line several times before going on to the next):

lāzem‿^{e}tr**ū**ḥ

lāzem‿^{e}tr**ū**ḥ‿^{e}tj**ī**b

lāzem‿^{e}tr**ū**ḥ‿^{e}tj**ī**b k**u**rsi

lāzem‿^{e}tr**ū**ḥ‿^{e}tj**ī**b k**u**rsi la-'**i**mmak

'ab**ū**y biq**ū**l inno **lā**zem‿^{e}tr**ū**ḥ‿^{e}tj**ī**b k**u**rsi la-'**i**mmak

Say each phrase slowly at first, then more quickly. Try this method of making up complex sentences for yourself. You'll find useful components in the lessons we've been studying: *it's not possible that ..., they told me that ..., a week ago they told me that ...*, etc. Good luck!

How to translate *no* and *not* into Arabic (summary)

No!	**la**' !
not with a verb in the past, present-future or subjunctive *not* with ^{c}**i**ndi… * (meaning *I've got*) *not* with b**i**ddi, b**i**ddak… *	ma… -š
not before any other word**	muš / miš
Neither ... nor ...	**la**… w**a**la… / **la**… wal**a**…

* Because, although they are not verbs, these words behave as if they were.

** *Not me, not nice, not now, not like that, not at home*, etc.

How would you declare a stock of 102 books to the Income Tax authorities in Arabic?

a. Actually, you will probably never have to;

b. And anyway, to avoid grammatical complications, you could just declare 100; but …

Now, seriously, let's learn how to say 101-110 books / children.
We know how to say *99 children*: **t**i**s**ᶜa u-tisᶜ**ī**n w**a**lad
We also know that 100 is m**i**yye. Now we can add *100 children*: m**ī**t w**a**lad,
I've told you 100 times! qult-**i**llak m**ī**t m**ɑ**rrɑ !

101	m**i**yye u-w**ā**ḥad	101 books	m**i**yye u-kt**ā**b (w-ᵉkt**ā**b)
102	m**i**yye u-tn**ē**n	102 books	m**i**yye u-ktāb**ē**n
103	m**i**yye u-tal**ā**te	103 books	m**i**yye u-t**a**lat k**u**tob

And so on, up to 110.
111-199 is like 11-99, with the addition of m**i**yye before the numbers 11-99:
187 children m**i**yye u-s**a**bᶜa u-taman**ī**n w**a**lad.

Summary of the Rules of Stress

z**a**-la-me, k**a**-ta-bu	Are all the syllables short?	The first syllable is stressed
s**ā**ken, bɑṭ**ɑ̄**le, kam**ā**n	Is there a **long** syllable?	The **long** syllable is stressed
taᶜbān**ī**n, sākn**ī**n	Are there **two long** syllables?	The **second** long syllable is stressed (and the first is shortened)
ka-t**a**b-t, ka-t**a**b-na jāb**a**t-li, ba-l**a**d-kom	Are there two consonants together without an intervening vowel?	The stress falls on the syllable before the consonant with no following vowel.

If there are several syllables in the word that have a "claim" to the stress according to the rules above, the **last** one "wins:"

ka - tab -	t**ī** - ha		lā -	z**e**m - na
consonant with no following vowel	long syllable		long syllable	consonant with no following vowel

That's **the secret of getting the stress right in colloquial Arabic**, and there are hardly any exceptions. It's the key to the rhythm of the language. Once again, remember that there's no need for you to overload your memory with these rules! They are here purely to satisfy your curiosity. By applying them daily you'll absorb them almost unconsciously.

Smile!

A student on a colloquial Arabic course once overheard two little girls aged 6-8 chatting and exclaimed in astonishment: "How wonderful! Such little girls and they know all the rules of correct stress!".

For perfectionists – transcription issues

The perfectionists among you may have found some things surprising. For example:

1. Stressed syllable

Why is the same word sometimes stressed and sometimes not? For example, š**ū** / šu, **ya**^{c}ni / ya^{c}ni. The answer is simple: that's how it sounds in the normal flow of conversation, and the transcription tries to be as authentic as possible. The differences lie in the intonation of the sentence. English behaves similarly. For example, there is a difference between the slow and accentuated way a lecturer would ask his students: *What do you know about this phenomenon?* and the colloquial expression of surprise: *Well, wh**at** d'ye kn**o**w!* In the latter expression, *do you* becomes a single sound that is skipped over without any emphasis.

Accordingly, we find in the Conversation in Lesson 2:
ya^{c}ni... il-y**ō**m... (ya is stressed)
fī^{h} š**u**ġ^{o}l, ya^{c}ni? (with the main stress on **fī**^{h}, a secondary stress on š**u-**, and the intonation staying low and "flat" on the word ya^{c}ni, which is just "thrown in," and remains unstressed.)

The same could be said of the word š**ū**? on its own (long and stressed), in comparison with the combination šu **bi**ddak? šu is short and unstressed here, because the stress is on the following syllable **bi-**

These variations in stress are natural and are produced automatically in the flow of speech without any particular effort. The explanation is provided here purely to reassure anyone who has been bothered by these transcription anomalies.

2. Doubled consonants

A similar case of "authentic transcription" occurs when a consonant is doubled. The doubling is clearly heard when the doubled consonant is followed by a vowel. In **Lesson 6, Explanations 1**, we showed how the doubling was weakened and often disappeared if the doubled consonant were not followed by a vowel. It's easy enough to say b**i**ddak (b**i**d-dak), but the combination b**i**dd-kom is pronounced b**i**d-kom, with no doubling of the d-. When this happens, the transcription leaves out the doubling. We'll remind you of this again whenever such cases occur.

3. Hamza – the glottal stop

In words beginning with the letter '-, there is one specific case in which we don't transcribe the *hamza* ('):

– When the word beginning with ' **follows a vowel** (*a, e, i, o, u*). This is because the hamza is in most cases hardly heard:

b**i**ddi‿ar**ū**ḥ '**i**ḥna u-**i**ntu / w-**i**ntu

– On the other hand, **after a consonant**, the glottal stop should be pronounced clearly:

k**ī**f '**i**nte? – min '**i**mmak – mašġ**ū**l '**a**ktɑr, etc

Key to the Exercises

Here are the solutions to the exercises. When you finish each lesson compare your answers (the written ones, of course) with the key below. After you've corrected any mistakes, read the amended text out loud.

Lesson 1

1. This is a new house, and this is a new house, too.
2. Who lives in your house?
3. Do you live here, too?
4. That's not big
5. Who else lives here?
6. '**i**nte s**ā**ken fi ḥ**ē**fa? '**a**na kam**ā**n s**ā**ken fi ḥ**ē**fa.
7. J**ō**rj fi b**ē**tak? – **la'**, J**ō**rj muš fi b**ē**ti.
8. h**ā**da jd**ī**d. – **la'**, h**ā**da muš‿ejd**ī**d.
9. **bi**nto s**ā**kne fi b**ē**t‿ejd**ī**d, u-**bi**ntak kam**ā**n s**ā**kne fi b**ē**t‿ejd**ī**d.
10. '**a**na s**ā**ken fi b**ē**t il-mud**ī**r.
11. '**i**nti muš s**ā**kne h**ō**n.
12. il-b**ē**t miš ḥ**i**lu.
13. m**ī**n h**ā**di / m**ī**n h**ā**y?
14. h**ā**di muš **bi**ntak?
15. **la'**, h**ā**di miš **bi**nti.
16. ya Maryam w**ē**n **bi**ntek?
17. il-mud**ī**r muš fi b**ē**tak.
18. h**ā**y mad**ī**ne ḥ**i**lwe.
19. **bi**nto muš ḥ**i**lwe.
20. h**ā**da muš‿ejd**ī**d.

If you feel like doing an additional exercise, we've got a simple suggestion for you: translate sentences 1-5 above back into Arabic. The key, of course, is in Exercise A at the end of Lesson 1.

Lesson 2

1. My neighbor has children.
2. My children are at your neighbor's.
3. I haven't got a daughter.

4. I only have a son.
5. Your daughter's got money.
6. Yusef has a son.
7. The boy [is] at Yusef's.
8. yā Maryam k**ī**f ḥ**ā**lek?
9. '**a**na muš mɑbs**ū**ṭ il-y**ō**m.
10. il-jir**ɑ̄**n fi b**ē**tak?
11. l**a**', il-jir**ɑ̄**n miš ᶜ**i**ndi.
12. š**ū** fīʰ fi-r-r**ɑ̄**dyo‿l-y**ō**m?
13. il-y**ō**m ma f**ī**-š r**ɑ̄**dyo.
14. w**ē**n M**a**ryam, u-Y**ū**sef w**ē**no?
15. h**u**wwe fi-š-š**u**ġᵒl.
16. Y**ū**sef ᶜ**i**ndo ul**ā**d.
17. l**a**', Y**ū**sef ma ᶜind**ō**-š ul**ā**d.
18. w**ē**n jir**ɑ̄**nak / jir**ɑ̄**nek?
19. il-w**a**lad muš ᶜ**i**ndi.
20. w**ē**n b**ē**t jir**ɑ̄**nek?
21. ma ᶜind**ī**-š d**a**rs il-y**ō**m.
22. h**ā**da muš mɑẓb**ū**ṭ (or simply:) muš mɑẓb**ū**ṭ.
23. '**a**na kam**ā**n ᶜ**i**ndi mɑṣ**ɑ̄**ri.
24. '**i**nte kam**ā**n ᶜ**i**ndak b**ē**t ḥ**i**lu.
25. w**ē**n il-mɑṣ**ɑ̄**ri? muš ᶜ**i**ndak?
26. l**a**', il-mɑṣ**ɑ̄**ri fi-l-b**ē**t.
27. il-mɑṣ**ɑ̄**ri ᶜ**i**nd il-jir**ɑ̄**n.
28. ma f**i**šš ᶜ**i**ndi r**ɑ̄**dyo / ma ᶜind**ī**-š r**ɑ̄**dyo. f**ī**ʰ r**ɑ̄**dyo ᶜ**i**nd il-jir**ɑ̄**n.

Lesson 3

1. I'm tired today.
2. You're not tired, the work here isn't hard.
3. This work is very hard.
4. She's very tired from her job.
5. Maryam, are you busy now?
6. No, I'm not busy.
7. Where do your children live?
8. They live in Haifa.
9. Is there work in Haifa?

10. Yes, there's a lot of work.
11. Is **your** work hard <you, your work hard>?
12. Yes, and **your** work is pleasant / nice.

13. h**u**wwe mɑbs**ū**ṭ min š**u**ġlak.
14. h**i**yye miš mɑbs**ū**ṭɑ min š**u**ġlak.
15. m**ī**n hal-b**i**nt? miš b**i**nt‿il-mud**ī**r?
16. f**ī**^{h} h**ō**n n**ā**s. h**u**mme jir**ɑ̄**n-kom?
17. l**a**', muš jir**ɑ̄**n-na.
18. h**ā**da š**u**ġl‿^{e}mn**ī**ḥ.
19. il-w**a**lad b**ɑ**rrɑ ma^{c} il-b**i**n^{e}t.
20. w**ē**n sākn**ī**n ul**ā**dak?
21. fi b**ē**t-hom (b**ē**t-hen^{G}).
22. u-had**ō**l, w**ē**n sākn**ī**n?
23. miš fi-l-b**ē**t h**ā**da.
24. jir**ɑ̄**n-kom mɑbsūṭ**ī**n min š**u**ġli?
25. mɑbsūṭ**ī**n‿^{e}kt**ī**r!
26. ewl**ā**d-na miš b**ɑ**rrɑ? – l**a**', h**u**mme (h**e**nne) fi-l-b**ē**t.
27. l**a**', halq**ē**t h**u**mme // issa h**e**nne ^{c}ind il-jir**ɑ̄**n.
28. il-jir**ɑ̄**n mɑbsūṭ**ī**n min ir-r**ɑ̄**dyo… '**a**na l**a**'!
29. had-d**a**rs ṣ**ɑ**^{c}eb, '**a**na ta^{c}b**ā**n / ta^{c}b**ā**ne.
30. ṭ**ɑ**yyeb, bik**a**ffi!

Lesson 4

1. This book's good.
2. Where's the new house?
3. Your daughter wants money.
4. We don't want exercise books! Everyone's got an exercise book, [that's] enough. We only want books.
5. Do you have books?
6. No we don't.

7. b**i**nti kb**ī**re.
8. b**i**nto kam**ā**n‿^{e}kb**ī**re.
9. b**i**ddi kt**ā**b.
10. b**i**ddi kam**ā**n‿^{e}kt**ā**b.
11. š**u**ġli mn**ī**ḥ.
12. mɑẓb**ū**ṭ, š**u**ġlak‿^{e}mn**ī**ḥ.

13. h**ā**da ktīr!
14. l**a**', h**ā**da muš‿^{e}ktīr.
15. h**u**wwe s**ā**ken ma^c '**i**bno fi-l-b**ē**t ij-jd**ī**d / fi-l-b**ē**t l-^{e}jd**ī**d.
16. minš**ā**n '**ē**š b**i**d-ha mαṣ**ᾱ**ri ?
17. ma^c m**ī**n il-ḥ**a**qq? – il-ḥ**a**qq m**a**^{c}i!
18. '**a**na muš mαbs**ū**ṭ m**i**nnak.
19. hal-w**a**lad ^{c}**i**ndo k**u**tob u-daf**ā**ter, u-h**ā**da bik**a**ffi minš**ā**n il-m**a**drase.
20. b**i**ntak b**i**dha kam**ā**n‿^{e}kt**ā**b? – l**a**', ma bidh**ā**-š.
21. b**i**dkom š**u**ġ^{o}l w**i**lla mαṣ**ᾱ**ri?
22. m**ā** b**i**dna / ma bidn**ā**-š mαṣ**ᾱ**ri, b**i**dna š**u**ġ^{o}l.
23. f**ī**^{h} h**ō**n m**a**drase kb**ī**re.
24. ^{c}**i**ndak mαṣ**ᾱ**ri 'aktαr m**i**nni.
25. h**ā**da minš**ā**ni.
26. '**a**ywa, h**ā**da minš**ā**nek.
27. ^{c}**i**ndo mαṣ**ᾱ**ri 'aktαr min k**u**ll il-jir**ᾱ**n.
28. halq**ē**t // '**i**ssa ma ^{c}ind**ī**-š w**a**q^{e}t.
29. ^{c}**i**ndi bass‿^{e}kt**ā**b‿^{e}zġ**ī**r.
30. '**a**na ta^{c}b**ā**n! – ta^{c}b**ā**n min '**ē**š?

Lesson 5

1. Maryam, you've got to bring a chair.
2. Do you want me to bring another chair?
3. No, there's no need.
4. Come and see us with your sister <come to at us….>.
5. He's got a good job, and he brings money home every day.
6. Do you want to go? / Don't you want to go?
7. Yes I do, I want to go with him.
8. I want to bring money to my mother, too.

9. l**ā**zem ij**ī**b id-dokt**ō**r.
10. '**i**ssa / halq**ē**t bij**ī**b il-jar**ī**de.
11. l**ā**zem iš**ū**f il-m**a**drase.
12. b**i**ddo‿ir**ū**ḥ la-^{c}ind il-jir**ᾱ**n.
13. b**u**krα bir**ū**ḥ ^{c}a-l-m**a**drase.
14. l**ē**š b**i**ddak‿^{e}tr**ū**ḥ la-hun**ā**k?
15. b**i**ddek‿^{e}tš**ū**fi b**i**ntek?
16. b**u**krα b^{e}tš**ū**fi b**i**ntek.

17. yā Yūsef, rūḥ la-ᶜind ’immak. – ya mᾱmα, fūti ᶜa-l-bēt!
18. hallaq lāzem ’arūḥ ᶜa-l-madrase.
    bukrα barūḥ ᶜa-l-madrase.
19. biddak‿ᵉtšūf binti? hiyye muš fi-l-bēt.
20. ya Maryam, biddek‿ᵉtrūḥi maᶜna ᶜa-l-madrase?
    – la’, barūḥ baᶜdēn.
21. lēš? – li’anno ’ana mašġūle.
22. ya walad, miš lāzem‿ᵉtfūt ᶜala bēt il-jirᾱn.
23. il-ḥaqq maᶜo.
24. mā biddi arūḥ / ma biddī-š ’arūḥ ᶜa-l-madrase.
    biddi arūḥ ᶜala ḥēfa.
25. ṭαyyeb, rūḥ maᶜ ’uḫtak ᶜala ḥēfa, u-jib-li jarīde min hunāk.
26. muš lāzem išūf hāda ᶜa-ṭ-ṭᾱwle.

Lesson 6

1. You go in, I’ll go in later.
2. The boy doesn’t want to go in.
3. Yes he does. He wants to go in with his sister.
4. Now he’s going to see <he will go to at> his paternal uncle Khalil.
   – Do you want to go, too?
5. No, I’m busy now, I’ll go tomorrow.
6. The children want to go to the cinema.
7. If you go, I’ll go with you.
8. ’iza bišūf hāda, bikūn mαbsūṭ, u-inti
   ’iza bᵉtšūfi hāda, bᵉtkūni mαbsūṭα.
9. bukrα l-ewlād bikūnu mαbsūṭīn, li’anno ma fī-š madrase.
   ’ana kamān bakūn mαbsūṭ, li’anno ma fī-š dars.
10. Yūsef sāken fi-n-nᾱṣre u-Maryam sākne fi-l-quds.
11. biddi arūḥ ᶜa-n-nᾱṣre u-hiyye bid-ha‿trūḥ ᶜa-l-quds.
12. bukrα barūḥ kamān mαrrα.– ṭαyyeb, jib-li kamān wāḥad.
13. bukrα lāzem‿ᵉnrūḥ ᶜa-l-madrase, w-il-yōm kamān.
14. muš lāzem‿ᵉtrūḥ hallaq, bᵉtrūḥ bukrα.
15. lāzem‿ᵉnrūḥ min hōn ᶜašān‿ikūn mαbsūṭ.
16. ’aḥsan‿ᵉtrūḥ la-ᶜindo hallaq, li’anno huwwe mαrīḍ.
17. jīb ir-rᾱdyo la-hōn ḥatta‿l-jirᾱn ikūnu mαbsūṭīn.
18. ’iza bᵉtjīb ir-rᾱdyo, bikūnu mαbsūṭīn.

19. muš lāzem‿^{e}tjīb l-^{e}ktāb la-hōn.
20. mā biddo‿irūḥ ^{c}a-l-quds, biddo‿irūḥ ma^{c}na ^{c}ala ḥēfa.
21. biddak‿^{e}trūḥ ^{c}a-n-nāṣre?
22. 'aywa, 'ibni fi-l-madrase fi-n-nāṣre.
23. 'iza bifūt, 'ana bafūt ma^{c}o.

Lesson 7

1. Whose is this book?
2. He hasn't got the key [on him].
3. Look, the key's in the door.
4. The chair's beside the window.
5. Where are your sisters? They're in the kitchen.
6. I want to see your big sister before ten o'clock.
7. I've got work for her.
8. Fine, I'll tell her.
9. There's no sun today.
10. What color is the bus <what [is the] color-of the bus>? – Which bus? There's a red bus and a blue bus!
11. Move [away] from the window! I want to see the sun.

12. šū lōn il-bāb?
13. šū lōn bāb il-bēt?
14. jib-li jarīde qab^{e}l-ma‿trūḥ.
15. 'ēmta biddak‿^{e}trūḥ ^{c}a-l-madrase?
16. miš mumken irūḥ hallaq, mā fī^{h} bāṣ.
17. fī^{h} hōn zalame, biddo išūfek.
18. 'ēš biddo minni, haz-zalame?
19. biqūl inno muftāḥ il-madrase ma^{c}ek.
20. muš maẓbūṭ, il-muftāḥ ^{c}ala-ṭ-ṭāwle, fi-l-maṭbaḫ.
21. iṭ-ṭāwle illi fi-l-maṭbaḫ…
22. il-kursi barra fi-š-šams.
23. il-karāsi illi fi-l-madrase.
24. jīb il-jarāyed illi ^{c}a-ṭ-ṭāwle.
25. šūf 'iza‿l-busuklēt / l-baskalēt barra willa juwwa.
26. bikaffi, 'ana ta^{c}bān(e) min had-dars.

(What about the "sun letters"?)

27.	il-k**u**rsi	il-mɑṣ**ɑ̄**ri	iṭ-ṭ**ɑ̄**wle	il-f**i**krɑ
28.	il-mɑr**ī**ḍ	id-d**a**ftɑr	il-m**a**drase	in-n**ā**s
29.	iz-z**a**lame	il-m**ɑ**ṭbɑḫ	is-s**ē**^{c}a	id-d**ɑ̄**r

Lesson 8

1. This is the same key.
2. This is the man who wrote the letter.
3. Where's the boy who hit you?
4. He goes into the neighbors' house.
5. This woman is going to the cinema with her husband.
6. My mother lives there alone, poor thing.
7. You must visit her every day.
8. My brother's not here <not present>. He left the house this morning <today the morning>.

9. ’**i**ḥna sākn**ī**n fi n**a**fs‿il-b**ē**t.
10. il-y**ō**m kam**ā**n k**a**tab n**a**fs‿il-makt**ū**b.
11. ’**i**nti kat**a**bti‿l-makt**ū**b la-ḥ**ā**lek?
12. ’**i**nte kat**a**bt‿il-makt**ū**b la-ḥ**ā**lak?
13. ’**a**ywa, ’**a**na kat**a**bto la-ḥ**ā**li.
14. ’**a**na ṭɑl**ɑ**b^{e}t d**a**ftɑr ’**a**zrɑq u-h**ū** ṭ**ɑ**lɑb n**a**fs‿iš-š**ī**.
15. y**a**^{c}ni n**a**fs‿id-d**a**ftɑr ^{e}b-n**a**fs‿il-l**ō**n.
16. ’**i**mmi ṭ**ɑ**lbat mɑṣ**ɑ̄**ri min ’ab**ū**y.
17. b**i**ddo ir**ū**ḥ ^{c}ala ḥ**ē**fa u-iz**ū**r ^{c}**a**kka fi n**a**fs‿il-y**ō**m.
18. h**u**wwe s**a**’al ’**i**mmi, ’**i**mmi s**a**’lat ’ab**ū**y.
19. (h**i**yye) s**a**’lato, bass h**u**wwe s**a**kat.
20. (h**u**wwe) s**a**’al ’**u**ḫti ’**i**za f**ī**^{h} ḥal**ī**b fi-l-m**ɑ**ṭbɑḫ.
21. sa’**a**lt il-w**a**lad: qadd**ē**š ^{c}**u**mrak?
22. j**ɑ̄**rna ḍ**ɑ**rɑb ’**i**bno.
23. sa’**a**lna j**ɑ̄**rna l**ē**š ḍ**ɑ**rɑb ’**i**bno.
24. – ^{e}mb**ē**reḥ mar**a**qtu jamb b**ē**tna.
25. – mɑẓb**ū**ṭ, mar**a**qna fi-š-š**ā**re^{c} u-sa’**a**lna w**ē**n ’**i**ntu sākn**ī**n.
26. šū l**ō**n b**ā**b il-b**ē**t?

Lesson 9

1. I've got two children, a boy and a girl.
2. How old is the boy <the boy, how much his age>? – A year and a half.
3. And the girl, how old is she?
4. Five <years>.
5. He passed by here an hour ago <before an hour>.
6. My mother isn't here <not present>. Would you like to see my father?
7. Is there someone outside?
8. We live in the same house.
9. He left the bicycle beside the storeroom.
10. ḥ**a**da ṭ**ɑ**lɑb m**i**nnak il-muft**ā**ḥ?
11. l**a**', ma-ḥad**ā**-š ṭ**ɑ**lɑb m**i**nni '**i**ši.
12. j**ɑ̄**rna s**a**'alak w**ē**n 'ab**ū**k? – l**a**', s**a**'al '**i**mmi.
13. sa'**a**lna‿l-muḫt**ɑ̄**r '**i**za fī^{h} b**ɑ̄**ṣ, q**ā**l : m**ā**-fī^{h}.
14. '**ē**š ṭɑl**ɑ**btu m**i**nni‿mb**ē**reḥ?
15. biq**ū**l inno '**i**nte (or: biq**ū**l innak) '**i**bn‿il-muḫt**ɑ̄**r.
16. h**ā**da l^{e}-kt**ā**b, šu ḥ**a**qqo?
17. '**i**ssa m**a**raq il-b**ɑ̄**ṣ.
18. ma-ḥad**ā**-š m**a**raq min h**ō**n.
19. m**ī**n k**a**tab hal-makt**ū**b?
20. ma-ḥad**ā**-š k**a**tab la-'ab**ū**y.
21. ṭɑl**ɑ**b^{e}t m**i**nno mɑṣ**ɑ̄**ri. – ṭ**ɑ**lɑb m**i**nha mɑṣ**ɑ̄**ri.
22. b**i**ddak q**a**hwe?
23. h**a**llaq ma bidd**ī**-š q**a**hwe, b**i**ddi ar**ū**ḥ.
24. haz-z**a**lame ᶜ**a**qlo kb**ī**r.
25. d**ā**yman biq**ū**l: ma bidn**ā**-š‿^{e}ṣy**ɑ̄**ḥ u-ṭ**ō**še.
26. b**i**dna sal**ā**m h**ō**n u-fi k**u**ll il-ᶜ**ā**lam.

Lesson 10

1. That's a beautiful story.
2. How was the film? Did you like it <did it please you>?
3. It's <this [is]> a new film, but I didn't like it.
4. We saw a better <more beautiful> film a week ago.
5. Every day he tells the same story.
6. Have you got relatives in Jerusalem?

7. No, but I've got a lot of friends.
8. She wanted to visit her mother.
9. j**i**b^{e}t ḥal**ī**b min ^{c}ind '**i**mmi.
10. h**u**wwe z**ɑ̄**r-ni u-**a**na z**u**rto.
11. biz**ū**rni kt**ī**r u-**a**na baz**ū**ro kam**ā**n.
12. yaY**ū**sef, šu q**u**lt? ya M**a**ryam, šu q**u**lti?
13. r**ū**ḥ m**a**^{c}o h**a**llaq ('**i**ssa / halq**ē**t).
14. ṣ**ɑ̄**ḥbak r**ɑ̄**ḥ m**a**^{c}ak ^{c}a-s-s**ī**nama?
15. '**a**ywa, '**a**na ru**ḥ**^{e}t m**a**^{c}o ^{c}a-s-s**ī**nama.
16. '**i**mmi r**ɑ̄**ḥat ma^{c} '**u**ḫti u-š**ā**fat il-f**i**l^{e}m.
17. ya M**a**ryam, ^{c}**a**jabek il-f**i**l^{e}m?
18. '**a**ywa, ^{c}aj**a**b-ni kt**ī**r.
19. h**ā**y ḫ**ā**mes m**ɑ**rrɑ biz**ū**rni.
20. šu q**a**l-lak?
21. q**a**l-li: r**ū**ḥ m**a**^{c}o, '**a**na bar**ū**ḥ ba^{c}d**ē**n.
22. ^{c}**i**ndi qɑr**ɑ̄**yeb fi ḥ**ē**fa.
23. u-**a**na ^{c}**i**ndi‿ṣḥ**ɑ̄**b fi ^{c}**a**kka.
24.ya Jam**ī**le, šu q**u**lti la-l-w**a**lad?
25. j**ā**b‿^{e}mlabbas la-'**u**ḫto.
26. '**i**nte ḍ**ē**f-na.
27. '**i**ntu ḍy**ū**f-na.
28. '**u**ḫti j**ā**bat b**i**n^{e}t (b**i**nt).
29. '**u**ḫti ^{c}**i**ndha b**i**n^{e}t
30. '**ē**š b**i**ddak kam**ā**n?

Lesson 11

1. š**u**f^{e}t 'aḫ**ū**k? – '**a**ywa, š**u**fto.
2. ya n**ā**s, š**u**ftu 'aḫ**ū**y? – '**a**ywa, šufn**ā**^{h}.
3. il-jir**ɑ̄**n š**ā**fu b**i**ntak? – '**a**ywa, š**ā**f**ū**-ha.
4. in-n**ā**s b**i**d-hom iš**ū**fu‿l-f**i**l^{e}m. – '**a**ywa, b**i**dhom išūf**ū**^{h}.
5. '**i**mmak š**ā**fat il-k**a**lb? – '**a**ywa, š**ā**fato.
6. jibtu‿l-jarīde? – '**a**ywa, jibn**ā**-ha.
7. f**ī**^{h} n**ā**s wɑr**ɑ̄**y? – '**a**ywa, f**ī**^{h} n**ā**s wɑr**ɑ̄**k / wɑr**ɑ̄**ki.
8. l**ā**zem aj**ī**b il-b**i**nt? – '**a**ywa, l**ā**zem‿^{e}tjīb-ha / ^{e}tjīb**ī**-ha.
9. l**ā**zem‿^{e}nz**ū**r il-m**a**tḥaf ? – '**a**ywa, l**ā**zem‿^{e}tzūr**ū**^{h} '**i**ntu kam**ā**n.

10. il-ḥ**a**qq ^{c}ala‿l-jir**ā**n? – '**a**ywa, il-ḥ**a**qq ^{c}al**ē**-hom (-hen).
11. il-ḥ**a**qq ^{c}al**ē**ha! – **la**', il-ḥ**a**qq ^{c}al**ē**k (± '**i**nte).
12. il-ul**ā**d k**a**tabu‿d-d**a**rs ? – '**a**ywa, katab**ū**^{h}.
13. u-**i**nte kam**ā**n kat**a**bt id-d**a**rs? – '**a**ywa, kat**a**bto.
14. il-b**i**nt illi šufn**ā**-ha fi-l-m**a**drase.
15. il-m**a**blaġ illi dafa^{c}n**ā**^{h}‿emb**ē**reḥ.
16. il-m**a**drase illi (il-m**a**drase‿lli) zurn**ā**-ha.
17. il-jar**ī**de illi (il-jar**ī**de‿lli) jibt**ī**-ha.
18. il-f**i**l^{e}m illi š**ā**fato.

Lesson 12

1. l**ā**zem t**i**ftaḥi.
2. b**i**ddi **a**dfa^{c}: b**a**dfa^{c}.
3. hal-m**a**blaġ, b**a**dfa^{c}o.
4. l**ā**zem y**i**s'al.
5. b^{y}**i**s'al (b**i**s'al) il-mud**ī**r.
6. b**i**s'alo.
7. liss**ā**-k h**ō**n (liss**ā**tak h**ō**n) / b**a**^{c}dak^{G} h**ō**n?
8. liss**ā**-ki h**ō**n / b**a**^{c}dek h**ō**n?
9. liss**ā**-hom (b**a**^{ce}d-hen) fi-l-m**a**tḥaf.
10. l**i**ssa ma fataḥ**ū**-š.
11. liss**ā**-ni (b**a**^{ce}d-ni) s**ā**ken fi n**a**fs‿il-b**ē**t.
12. Shall we send this letter? Yes, we'll send it. No, we won't send it.
13. Hey, Samira, did you ask the boss?
14. Why didn't you^{f} ask the boss?
15. You^{f} must ask him!
16. If I want to open [it], I'll open [it].
17. I want to open the door. I'll open it now / I'm opening it now.
18. You must not open [it]. Why do you open [it]?
19. What <with what> do you want to open [it] with? I want to open [it] with the key.
20. il-m**a**blaġ illi daf**a**^{c}to.
21. muš l**ā**zem t**i**dfa^{c} h**a**llaq.
22. sa'**a**lt 'ab**ū**k? – l**i**ssa (b**a**^{c}d).
23. ^{c}**ā**datan b**a**ftaḥ il-b**ā**b ḥ**a**tta‿if**ū**t.

24. bass hal-marra mā biddi (ma biddī-š) ’aftaḥ.
25. il-maktūb illi katabtū^{h}.
26. il-bāb illi fataḥto / illi fataḥnā^{h}.
27. kull yōm biftaḥ iš-šababīk.
28. biftaḥ il-bāb? – ’aywa, biftaḥo. / la’, ma biftaḥō-š.
29. mīn sa’alak / sa’alek? – lāzem yis’al ’immo.
30. muš lāzem tis’al.

Lesson 13

1. lēš biddak‿^{e}trūḥ?	Why do you want to go?
2. bitšūf‿^{e}mnīḥ min hōn?	Can you see well from here?
3. kull yōm‿^{e}btikteb darsak?	Do you write your lesson every day?
4. na^{c}am, kull yōm bakteb darsi.	Yes, every day I write my lesson.
5. ’ēš‿^{e}btuṭlob minno ?	What do you want <ask> from him?
6. baṭlob‿^{e}ktāb‿^{e}jdīd.	I want <ask for> a new book.

7. You must pay every month.
8. You don’t have to pay now. You can pay some other <another> time.
9. The cat^{f} ran away from home. What do you think of that <what do you say>?
10. Well, we’ve tied up the dog, [but] we can’t tie up the cat as well!

11. (huwwe) dafa^{c}? – la, lissa ma dafa^{ce}-š.
12. dāyman bidfa^{c}, bass il-yōm (ma) biddō-š yidfa^{c}.
13. ’iza bidfa^{c}, ^{e}mnīḥ. ’iza mā bidfa^{c} (ma bidfa^{ce}-š), bnikteb la-’immo.
14. Samīra btis’al qaddēš is-sē^{c}a.
15. hiyye btuṭlob minni maṣāri. – u-minni kamān talbat maṣāri.
16. ya walad, lēš‿^{e}btuḍrob l-ewlād fi-š-šāre^{c}?
17. ’ana? ma baḍrob-š (baḍrob^{e}-š) hada.
18. id-duḫḫān illi zara^{c}nā^{h}.
19. iḍ-ḍarībe illi (iḍ-ḍarībe‿lli) dafa^{c}tū-ha.
20. l-^{e}ḥsāb illi dafa^{c}to.
21. l-^{e}ḥsāb illi dafa^{c}tī^{h}.

Lesson 14

1. dahan**ū**^{h}.
2. dahan**ū**-ha
3. (–).
4. y**i**dhano.
5. badh**a**n-ha… tidhan-h**ā**-š
6. m**a**za^{c}o.
7. maza^{c}**ō**-š.
8. maz**a**^{c}-ha.
9. timza^{c}-h**ā**-š.
10. inno.
11. illi dah**a**n-ha.
12. (–).
13. illi maza^{c}**ū**^{h}.
14. ma rαk**α**ḍ-š.
15. ma rαkḍ**α**t-š
16. turk**o**ḍ-š.
17. (–).
18. b^{y}**i**jma^{c} / b**i**jma^{c}.
19. bijm**a**^{c}-hom.
20. (–)
21. ma bijma^{c}**ū**-š.

Lesson 15

1. His house is cleaner than yours <than your^{m} house>.
2. This is the cleanest house in the town.
3. This is the biggest egg.
4. That's a more attractive color, I like it better <it pleases me more>.
5. My daughter's married.
6. Who's your daughter's husband? And what's he like <how [is] he>?
7. There's no difference between the two.
8. You^{m} are wrong! No, it's you^{f} who's wrong <you [are] the-mistaken-one>.
9. We all saw the film, apart from Yusef.
10. He's never paid taxes in his life <his lifetime he didn't pay taxes>.

11. ^{c}umri ma ruḥt^{e}-š ^{c}a-s-sīnama.
12. kam marra šuf^{e}t hal-fil^{e}m?
13. qaddēš biddak tidfa^{c}?
14. fī^{h} bin^{e}t 'akbar minnek?
15. mīn 'akbar wāḥad?
16. huwwe 'akbar minni b-šahrēn.
17. fī^{h} ^{c}indo ṭawābe^{c} 'aktar minni.
18. il-yōm id-dars 'aṭwal.
19. la', miš 'aṭwal, nafs‿iš-šī.
20. ^{e}mbala, hāda dars ṭawīl‿^{e}ktīr.

21. qaddēš ^{c}umrak?
22. u-ibnak, qaddēš ^{c}umro?
23. kam sane // sine kunt ^{c}indo?
24. kam wāḥad fī^{h} ^{c}in(d)kom?
25. mīn 'akbar wāḥad, 'inte willa huwwe?
26. huwwe 'akbar minni, bass 'ana 'aṭwal minno.
27. kam marra kunt (kun^{e}t) hunāk?
28. walad 'ašṭar ^{c}umri ma šuft^{e}-š.
29. kam ^{c}ēle fī^{h} fi-l-balad.
30. muš 'aktar min sab^{c}īn.
31. mīn kān 'āḫer wāḥad (wāḥed)?
32. mā fī^{h} far^{e}q bēn it-t^{e}nēn.
33. fataḥt‿id-dukkān‿^{e}mbēreḥ?
34. biddi wāḥed 'aḥla.
35. biddi 'aḥla wāḥad.
36. ^{c}indo kutob 'akbar.
37. hāda 'akbar‿^{e}ktāb.
38. 'ēš il-far^{e}q bēn l-^{e}ktābēn?
39. biqūlu (± inno) fī^{h} farq‿^{e}kbīr.

Revision exercise on the subjunctive:

1. ḥatta‿tšūf 'aḫūk.
2. mīn qal-lak inno b^{e}tšūf 'aḫūk bukra?
3. muš lāzem‿išūfek.
4. biqūl inno bišūfek bukra.
5. ḥatta‿izūru‿l-matḥaf.

6. m**ī**n q**a**l-lak inno biz**ū**ru ^{c}**a**mmi?
7. muš l**ā**zem y**i**b^{c}at il-makt**ū**b h**a**llaq.
8. biq**ū**l inno b**i**b^{c}ato ba^{c}d**ē**n.
9. miš l**ā**zem y**i**dfa^{c} k**u**ll il-m**a**blaġ.
10. biq**ū**l b**i**dfa^{c} b**u**krɑ.
11. m**ī**n q**a**l-lak b**i**dfa^{c} kull š**a**h^{e}r?
12. ḥ**a**tta t**i**dfa^{c} n**a**fs‿il-m**a**blaġ.
13. m**ī**n q**a**l-lak bik**ū**nu fi-l-b**ē**t?
14. ḥ**a**tta‿ik**ū**nu mɑbsūṭ**ī**n.
15. muš l**ā**zem ik**ū**nu fi n**a**fs‿il-m**a**drase.
16. biq**ū**l inno bik**ū**nu ^{c}**i**ndak b**u**krɑ.

Index of Vocabulary and Rules

Notes:
- 12 = Lesson 12
- 15-17 = Lesson 15, footnote 17.
- 8-e-2 = Lesson 8, Explanations 2.

The ᶜ, which has no English equivalent, appears in this list as the first letter of the alphabet. For example, the word maᶜqūl will appear earlier in the list than the word mablaġ.

C
ᶜā'ile 15
ᶜādatan 12
ᶜāde 12
ᶜajab 10-11
ᶜajan 13
ᶜala 5
ᶜala, ᶜalē- 11-e-2
ᶜālam 9
ᶜām 12-8
ᶜamm 6
ᶜan 7, 15-14
ᶜaql, ᶜaqᵉl 9
ᶜāšer 9-e-3
ᶜēle 15
ᶜind 2, 5-e-4
ᶜumri 15, 15-5

A
'ā 1
'aᶜma 10
'ab, 'abu 7
'abṣαr 11-2
'abu (Yūsef...) 9-e-2
'abū-y, -k 11, 11-e-1, p. 75
adjective 1-e-4,
'ahl 4-4
'ahla, 'ahlan 4, 4-4, 6-6
'aḥmar 7
'aḥsan 6
'aḥsan-ma 13-4
'aḫ 7
'aḫad 8
'aḫad waqᵉt 11-3
'āḫer 15
'aḫras 10
'aḫu 7
'aḫūy 7, 11-e-1
'ajīb? 11-4
'akal 11
'akam/ akam 15-e-1
'akbαr 12
'akbαr walad 15-e-2
'aktαr 12
all of us 15-e-5
'αllα 6-6
'αllᾱh 6-6
'amērka 8
'ana 1
'αrḍ 12
attached pronouns 1-e-6
'awlād 2-9
'awwal 9-e-3
'awwal‿embāreḥ 10
'awwal‿embēreḥ 10
'awwalt‿embēreḥ 10-7

'aywa 1
'ayy, 'ayya 7, 7-4
'azraq 7

B
b- 8-2
b^{c}īd 15
ba^{c}at 12
ba^{c}ed (after) 6
ba^{c}ed (yet) 12-12,12-e-3
bα^{c}eḍ 15
ba^{c}dēn 5
bāb 7
bū̄bα 5
baby (have a -) 10-3
bakkīr 14-e-1
balad 12
balāš 5
bāqi 10
bαrrα 3, 7
baskalēt 7-2
bass 6-e-1
bū̄ṣ 6-11, 6-e-1
bαṭū̄le 3
be- 12-e-1
be (to be) 1, 1-e-1
bēḍα 15-e-1
bēn, bēnāt 15-e-4
biddi 4, 6-e-1
bid-henn^{e}š p.38
bijū̄z 11
bīk 4-5
bikaffi 1
bint 2 - bin^{e}t 3-e-2
bīrα 9
bukrα 6, 6-4

burdāy 7
bustān 11
busuklēt 7-2

C
comparative 10-e-2, 15

D
dafa^c 9
dafaš 14
daftαr 4
dahan 14
daḥal 9
dalīl 8
daqīqa 9
dū̄r 3, 3-1
dāyman 6
days 13-e-1
definite article 1, 2-e-1, 4-e-2
dinya 2
dīr bālak 13
doktōr 5
dual 9-e-2
duḫḫān 12-7
dukkān 14

Ḍ
ḍαrαb 8, 13
ḍαrībe 12, 13-e-2
ḍēf 10

E
e ḫtyū̄r - see ḫeṭyū̄r
'ēmta 6
'ēš 4, 4-e-4
ewlād 2-9, 15-7

F

fallāḥ 12
farq, fareq 15
fataḥ 12
feminine 9-e-4
fēn 13
fi 1
fīh 2
fikr 15
fikra 5
filem 10-10
fī-š 2
fišš 2
fōq 15, 15-16
fūt 4

G

give birth 10-3

Ġ

ġalṭān 15
ġasal 13
ġasīl 13
ġēr 10-e-3

H

hāda 1
hadāk 15-13
hādi 1
hadōl 3
hal- 3, 3-e-1
hallaq 6
halqēt 1-2
hamza p.[9], p. 110
haq-, haqṣar 15-3
harab 13
have 2, 7-e-1
hawa 12-5
hāy

hayy- 5, 11-e-3
hayyen 4, 4-8
hēk 2, 10-e-2, 15-16
helping vowels 2-e-2, 13-e-4
henne 3
here is 11-e-3
hī, hiyye 1
hiyyā- 5, 11-e-3
hōn 1
hū 2
humme 3
hunāk 5
huwwe 2
hwayyen 4-8

Ḥ

ḥabel 13
ḥabīb 3
ḥada 9
ḥadd (*besides*) 7
ḥadd (*anyone*) 9
ḥādes (-ṯ) 11, 14-9
ḥafaẓ 12
ḥākūra 11
ḥāl 2, 8-e-2
ḥamd 2, 2-4
ḥaqq 4, 4-3, 9-7
ḥaqq cala... 11
ḥarb 9
ḥaṣad 13
ḥatta 6
ḥēfa 1
ḥilu 1

ḫ

ḫabar 10
ḫabaz 13
ḫalaṣ 14-e-1

ḫāmes 9-e-3
ḫaṭar 13
ḫayyi 4-7
ḫēr 1, 4
ḫeṭyār 6, 6-3
ḫubz, ḫubez 9

I

'iben 4
'iḥna 3
il- 1, 2-e-1, 4-e-2
illi 7-e-3, 9-8, 11-e-4, 14-e-2
'imm 5
'imm Yūsef 9-e-2
'in šā 'allāh 6-7
indefinite article 1-e-2
inn- 7, 7-3, 9-12
inni, innak… 9-12
inno 7, 7-3
inšalla 6-7
'inte, 'inta 1
'inti 1
'intu 3
'issa 1-2
'iši 2
-iyyām 13-e-1
'iza 6-13

J

jāb 5
jabal 15
jābat 10-3
jamaᶜ 14
jamb 7
jār 2
jdīd 1
Jerusalem 6-e-4
jīb 5
jōz 8
jumᶜa 8
juwwa 7

K

kaᶜk 9-3
kalb 11
kam 15-e-1
kamān 1, 6-e-5
kān 6
kān biddo 10, 10-1
kān fīh 10
kā-š 4-2
kazzāb 14-2
kbīr 1, 7-7, 15-e-3
kibrīt 4
kīf 2
kīlo 15-e-1
kī-š 4-2
kizeb 14-e-1
ktāb 4
ktīr 3
kull 2, 4, 15-e-5
kullayāt 15-e-5
kūn 6
kursi 5-1
kūsa 12
kwayyes 5

L

l- 5-e-3, 5-e-4
la- 5-e-3, 5-e-4
la… wa-la 5-5, p.107
la' 1-e-7
laḥadd 12
lāken 11
lāzem 5-e-1
lēš 6
li'anno 6

lissa, lissāt- 12-12, 12-e-3
lōn 7

M
ma 2-e-4, 4, 12-e-2, p.107
mà… unstressed 10-5
ma ᶜada 15
ma ᶜalēš / ᶜalešš 5, 11-e-2
ma ḥada, ma-ḥadā-š 9
mā šā ʾallāh 15-10
maᶜ 3, 7-e-1
maᶜlūm 4
maᶜqūl 9
mablaġ 12
mabsūṭ 2
madīne 1
madrase 4, 9-11
mā ḍi 12-8
maḥaṭṭa 6
maḥzan 8
majra 12-5
majrūḥ 11
mākana, mākina 8
maktab 13
maktūb 8
malek 10
mā ma 7
manaᶜ 12
mara 8-7
marbūṭ 13-5
marḥaba 12-6
marra 10, 12
masa 4
masalan 14-9
maṣā ri 2

masculine 1-e-3
maskīn 8
maṣer 9
maṣri 9
mašġūl 3
matal 13, 14-9
matalan 14-9
matḥaf 11-6
maṭbaᶜa 14-8
maṭbaḫ 7
mawḍūᶜ 9
mawjūd 8
mayy 4
mazaᶜ 14
mazbūṭ 2
ᵉmbala 5-7
ᵉmbāreḥ 4, 4-e-3
ᵉmbēreḥ 4, 4-e-3
mīn 1
min 3, 4-e-1
minšān 4
miskīn 8
miš 1, 1-e-7, p.107
mitjawwez 15
mjawwaze 15
mlabbas 10
mnīḥ 2, 2-e-2, 4-e-3
months 13-e-1
mudīr 1
muftāḥ 7
muhemm 15
muḫṭār 7
mustašfa 11
muš 1, 1-e-7, p.107
mūt 6
myself 8-e-2

N
na^{c}am 1
nafs 8-e-2
nɑ̄ṣre/-rɑ 6
našɑr 13
nāšef 11
nḍīf 15
negation 1-e-7
^{e}nšɑllɑ 6-7
numbers 9-e-3
nuṣṣ 6

O
’ōḍa 5

P
plural 2-e-3
possessives 1-e-8
pronunciation 1-e-10, 6-e-1

Q
qab^{e}l (-ma) 6
qaddēš 15-e-1
qahwe 9
qalīl 6-9
qalīle (^{c}a-l-) 13
qannīne 14
qarīb 10, 15-3, 15-15
qɑṣīr 15
qatal 8
qawām, qawɑ̄m 5
quddām 11-e-1
quds (il-) 6-e-4
question 1-e-9
qūl 5, 7
quṣṣɑ 10

R
rɑbɑṭ 13
rɑ̄be^{c} 9-e-3
rɑ̄ḥ 5
rɑ̄ḥat‿^{e}tjīb 10-3
rɑkɑḍ 14
root p. 61
rozz 15-e-1
rūḥ 5-e-1

S
sa’al 8
sābe^{c} 9-e-3
sādes 9-e-3
sahl, sah^{e}l 4-4
sakat 8, 13
sāken, sākne 1
salām 6, 9
salāmtak 4
samaḥ 13, 13-e-3
same 8-e-2
sawa 6
sē^{c}a 6
see you! 9-e-1
-self 8-e-2
she 5-e-2
sīnama 10
stress 3-e-3, 14, 14-e-3, p.109
su’āl 14
subjunctive 5-e-1, 6-e-2, 11-4
sun letters 2-e-1, 4-e-2
superlative 15-e-2

Ṣ
ṣɑ^{c}b, ṣɑ^{ce}b 3
ṣɑbɑ̄ḥ 2, 8-3
ṣɑbi 10, 15
ṣɑ̄ḥeb 10
ṣɑlɑ 14-3
ṣɑ̄r 11

ṣubᵉḥ, ṣubᵒḥ 8, 8-3
ṣyā̄ḥ 8

Š
š, -š 12-e-2
šaᶜb 9
šahᵉr 12
šahᵉr [ušhor] 13-e-1
šams 7
šanta 14
šāreᶜ 8
šā̄ṭer 4, 15-17
šēkel 12
šī 4-9, 8-8
šu, šū 1, 4-e-4
šubbāk 7, 12
šuġᵒl 2
šwayy 5, 7

T
ta 10-12
taᶜāl 5
taᶜbān 3
taᶜl-aqullak 10-e-4
talāte 9-e-3
talattɑᶜšɑr p.90
tālet 9-e-3
talt 9-e-3
tamām 6, 15
tāmen 9-e-3
tāni 2, 4, 9-e-3, 10-e-1
taqrīban 13
tarak 8
tāseᶜ 9-e-3
tᵉnēn 9-e-3
tfɑḍḍɑl 4, 5-3
that 3-e-1, 7-e-3, 11-e-4

tintēn 9-e-3
tlat 9-e-3
tnɑᶜšɑr p.90
tnēn 9-e-3
to 5-e-3, 5-e-4
tuḥfe 11-6

Ṭ
ṭɑ̄beᶜ 14-8
ṭɑrīq 13
ṭɑ̄wle 5
ṭōše 8

U
'uḫt 5, 7
ulād 2-9
'umm 5
'usbūᶜ 8
'ustāz 9-2
-ušhor 13-e-1

V
verb 5-3-1

W
w- 1
wāḥad / wāḥed 7-4, 9-e-3
wāḥad / wāḥed (kam –) 15-e-1
wala 5-5, p.107
walad 2, 15-7
waqt, waqᵉt 4, 6-12
wɑrɑ 11
wɑrɑ̄-y, wɑrɑ̄-k 11
wēn 1
willa 4
winta 6
which 11-e-4
who 7-e-3, 11-e-4

Y

ʸi-, ʸu- 12-13, 13-1
ya 1
yaᶜni 2, 2-5, p.109
yɑllɑ 9-5
yamm 15-16
yimken 9
yirḥam 8
yōm 2

Z

zalame 7
zamān 6
zaraᶜ 12
zawj 10
zġīr 11
zīḥ 7
zōbaᶜa 13
zūr 6

As you reach the end of the first book

Here you are at the end of the first book. You've gone over all the material, more or less, you've learned a lot, and you can now say hundreds of extremely useful sentences. You may have forgotten some of the things you've studied – or think you have – but at least you've come into contact with these things and made a superficial acquaintance with them. A seed has been sown, and in due time it will grow.

This has been the first **and most difficult** stage: foreign sounds and new rules, which, though comparatively easy to understand, are hard to apply in the course of conversation. Nonetheless, if you've been conscientious about doing the exercises, all this material is stored away somewhere in your memory.

When you began this course of study you entered virgin territory: rocks had to be cleared away and foundations laid before you could start to build. In Book 2 you won't be starting from scratch; you'll be moving forward over familiar ground, and you'll be able to use the same methods to continue building: another verb, whose conjugation greatly resembles that of verbs you already know; and more new words, some of which will remind you of those you learned in Book 1. If you persevere and advance step by step, and don't allow yourself to be overwhelmed by everything you've still got to learn, you'll negotiate Book 2 safely – and more easily – than you did Book 1.

Good luck!

And what's waiting for you in Book 2?

a) New verb forms, but – no major surprises. After all, you've already acquired the basics of verb conjugation. The verbs we'll be learning soon are very useful ones: *to do, to know, to understand, to be able, to laugh, to speak, to forget, to begin, to come* – how have we managed to come so far without them? In Book 2 you'll make their acquaintance.

b) A general overview of the different verb forms. We'll be concentrating especially on Form 2, which will open new horizons.

c) Lots of new vocabulary and new turns of phrase (*if I were..., if only..., the more I...*), the days of the week, telling the time, and many more useful rules, all accompanied by a wealth of exercises that will turn the new material into a vehicle for self-expression.

In Books 3 and 4 we shall finish covering all the verb forms and get to know something about "educated Arabic" (the language used in debates and interviews). Later on you'll be able to broaden your vocabulary and practice what you've learned with the help of an additional book: **The Olive-Tree Dictionary**.

And of this excellent plan we have to say, of course " 'in šᾱ' αllᾱh !"